Last Train
to Cooperstown

The 2006 Baseball Hall of Fame Inductees

from the Negro League Baseball Era

Kevin L. Mitchell

ISBN: 978-1-61296-489-8

PUBLISHED BY BLACK ROSE WRITING

www.blackrosewriting.com

Printed in the United States of America

Suggested retail price $14.95

Last Train to Cooperstown is printed in Cambria

To my lovely wife Margaree who God used to plant the seed for this book in me and who helped it come to life through her persistent encouragement and unfailing belief in me.

Praise for Last Train to Cooperstown

In The Last Train readers get an introduction to the 17 Negro Leaguers inducted into the Hall of Fame in 2006. Author Kevin Mitchell does not want their stories to be forgotten or to fade away so he brings the reader the basic highlights so people can see that playing in the Negro Leagues did not make for lesser careers. These 17 players and owners are worthy of their recognition.
~**Leslie Heaphy**, Associate Professor, History, Kent State University

Santop, Torriente, Suttles, Wilkinson, Mackey, Pompez and Mendez and are not household baseball names. Even the most zealous fans do not know of these men, who were among 12 ball players and five owner/executives inducted into the National Baseball Hall of Fame in 2006. Historian Kevin Mitchell shares what I and other members of the selection committee knew about their solid Cooperstown credentials and worthiness for baseball immortality. Jump on board and discover the triumphs and tribulations of these legendary barrier breakers before their last whistle stop in Cooperstown. A must read for all students of the game.
~**Larry Lester**, co-chair of the "Negro Leagues Researchers & Authors Group" (NLRAG) for the National Baseball Hall of Fame selection committee

ACKNOWLEDGMENTS

I am deeply indebted to the authors of the following books which provided a wealth of information for this book: *Shade of Glory: The Negro Leagues and the Story of African American Baseball* by Lawrence D. Hogan, *The Complete Book of Baseball's Negro Leagues: The Other Half of Baseball History* by John B. Holway, *Black Stars: Negro League Pioneers* by John B. Holway, *Negro League Baseball: The Rise and Ruin of a Black Institution* by Neil Lanctot, *Black Baseball in Kansas City* by Larry Lester, *Black Baseball's National Showcase: The East-West All Star Game: 1933-1953* by Larry Lester, *I Was Right on Time: My Journey From the Negro League to the Majors* by Buck O'Neil, Steve Wulf, and David Conrads, *Only The Ball Was White* by Robert Peterson, *A Complete History of the Negro Leagues 1884 – 1955* by Mark Ribowsky, *The Autobiography of Monte Irvin* by James A. Riley and Monte Irvin , *Biographical Encyclopedia of the Negro Baseball Leagues* by James A. Riley, and *Beyond the Shadow of the Senators: The Untold Story of the Homestead Grays and the Integration of Baseball* by Brad Synder.

Also, in my researched I used the following periodicals: the *New York Times and* the *Washington Post* and the following web sites: the Baseball Hall of Fame - www.baseballhalloffame.org, the Negro League Baseball Players Association - www.nlbpa.com, and the Society For American Baseball Research - www.sabr.org.

CONTENTS

Last Train
to Cooperstown

INTRODUCTION

The Negro Leagues were the professional baseball leagues African Americans created during the first half of the Twentieth Century when due to racism they were not allowed to play Major League baseball. There was no written rule specifically keeping black players out and Major League club owners denied such discrimination existed. But everyone knew of the "invisible color line" that black and Hispanic players were not allowed to cross. Although a product of racial segregation, Negro League baseball produced many of the game's great players as it operated in the shadow of the Major Leagues.

Jackie Robinson broke through the color line in 1947 and began his successful Major League playing career with the Brooklyn Dodgers. With the line erased by Robinson and as more African Americans began playing in the Major Leagues, the eventual future end of Negro League baseball became obvious by the early 1950s. Instead of attending Negro League games, more and more black baseball fans began following former Negro League players in the Major Leagues. By the middle of the decade talented young African American players were bypassing the Negro Leagues and directly signing with Major League teams. The death of Negro League baseball came by the early 1960s due to economic problems caused by a declining fan base and a decreasing level of talent.

Twenty-four former Negro League players had been inducted into the National Baseball Hall of Fame by the year 2001: Jackie Robinson (1962), Roy Campanella (1969), Satchel Paige (1971), Josh Gibson (1972), Buck Leonard (1972), Monte Irvin (1973), James "Cool Papa" Bell (1974), Judy Johnson (1975), Oscar Charleston (1976), Ernie Banks (1977), Martin Dihigo (1977), John

"Pop" Lloyd (1977), Willie Mays (1979), Andrew "Rube" Foster (1981), Henry Aaron (1982), Ray Dandridge (1987), Leon Day (1995), Bill Foster (1996), Willie Wells (1997), Larry Doby (1998), Wilber "Bullet" Rogan (1998), "Smokey" Joe Williams (1999), Norman "Turkey" Stearnes (2000), and Hilton Smith (2001),

But this was not a true representation of Negro League baseball's contributions to the game and rectification was needed. A committee of baseball historians sponsored by Major League Baseball did a thorough review of the Negro League era. The lack of documented Negro League game summaries and statistics, the inconsistent coverage of games by black newspapers, and the blatant ignoring of Negro League baseball by white major newspapers made the committee's efforts difficult. However, based on the existing written history of that era and interviews of surviving players and other baseball people of that time, the committee recommended an additional 12 ballplayers and 5 owners/executives from the Negro Leagues for Hall of Fame induction in the class of 2006: Frank Grant, Pete Hill, Jose Mendez, Louis Santop, Ben Taylor, Andy Cooper, Cristobal Torriente, Raleigh Mackey, George Suttles, Raymond Brown, Jud Wilson, Willard Brown, Sol White, J. L. Wilkinson, Cumberland Posey, Effa Manley, and Alejandro Pompez.

Currently, the popularity of baseball in black communities is declining as social and economic obstacles are preventing inner city kids from participating in the sport. The number of African Americans playing professional baseball has decreased as more young black male athletes have turned to aspirations of making millions in professional basketball and football. While Major League Baseball through its Reviving Baseball in Inner Cities (RBI) program has been addressing this issue, African American attendance at Major League games has also declined. However, because of Negro League baseball's rich history and its everlasting impact on the game, African Americans still have deep, grounded roots in the game that cannot be severed despite the current trends.

The stories of the 2006 Hall of Fame inductees from Negro League baseball in this book are reminders of these deep roots. Reading the profiles of the inductees will give you a deeper understanding of Negro League baseball as not just a part of African American history, but you'll see it is imbedded into the fabric of Twentieth Century American history. In spite of racial and economic obstacles the 12 ballplayers inducted faced, their stories paint a picture of Negro League baseball as the foundation for today's black professional athlete in every sport. The stories of the five owner/executives inducted also paint a picture of Negro League baseball as an integral part of black communities the first half of the Twentieth Century.

The feats on the diamond of the 2006 inductees are not celebrated as contributions to Negro League lore as those of Satchel Paige, Josh Gibson, "Cool Papa" Bell and the other Negro League legends previously enshrined in the Hall. However, the baseball accomplishments of that year's inductees were worthy of Hall of Fame recognition.

The committee's recommendation resulted in the Hall of Fame's largest number of inductees from Negro League baseball in one year. However, did the recommendations unintentionally indicate that there are no others from the Negro Leagues worthy of Hall of Fame recognition? What about Henry Kimbro, CI Taylor, Bill Byrd, or "Buck" O'Neil? Is the Hall of Fame door now shut for Negro League baseball? As more information and statistics from that baseball era are discovered, will there be other Negro League inductees in the future? Hopefully yes, but certainly not as many in one year as 2006.

Visualize this imaginary scene. What if the 2006 inductees from the Negro Leagues had been all living and arrived for their Hall of Fame ceremony on one long train with their families and supporters? It would have been a celebration like no other. Symbolically in that scene and in reality at least for now, the 2006 inductees were on the last train to Cooperstown from Negro League baseball. This increases the historical necessity of their stories being told.

Chapter 1

A Short History of Negro League Baseball

The Early Years

The game of baseball sprouted from roots deep in America's past, the early 1800s. However, because of its' similarity to the British games of cricket and rounder, baseball's beginning cannot be claimed as 100% American. By the start of the 20th Century, the game's popularity had grown so much it was considered solely American and the journey of it becoming the national pastime had begun.

The attitude of African Americans about baseball also reflected the growth of the game's popularity. The formation of local teams grew in black communities out of group social activities in cities such as New York, Boston, Philadelphia, and Washington, D.C. before and after the Civil War. There is also evidence that slaves played the game in the antebellum south. But despite the growth of the game's popularity among African Americans, baseball's journey of becoming the national pastime for them contained roadblocks and dead end streets.

African Americans played in white organized professional baseball before 1890 despite racial barriers. The first was John W. "Bud" Fowler who in 1878 played with Lynn, Massachusetts in the International Association. Moses "Fleet" Walker became the first African American to play in the Major Leagues. Walker, in 1884, played with Toledo in the American Association which in 1901 became Major League Baseball's American League. In 1887 at least six African Americans played in the International League which was considered the highest level of organized minor league baseball at that time: Bud Fowler, Frank Grant, Robert Higgins, Rudolph Jackson, George Stovey, and Moses Walker. However, as the 20th Century began there were no African Americans playing white organized baseball.

The racial barriers African American players faced in early organized professional baseball were a carryover of the overall racial prejudice in American society they experienced as the new century began. They faced it in every part of their lives and there was no difference in the sport that was becoming America's favorite. There was no written policy specifically banning black players and Judge Kenesaw Landis, Major League Baseball's first commissioner continually insisted no such rule or policy existed. But the truth was that black players were not allowed to play because of the color of their skin. Everyone knew there was an "invisible color line" they could not cross.

African Americans loved the game and their desire to play it gave birth to a number of black professional teams such as the Cuban Giants, Cuban X Giants, Chicago Union Giants, Philadelphia Giants, Page Fence Giants, and others. Several black leagues were organized, but none operated long enough to be historically recognized formally as official. Black teams were independent of any league and played not only local games, but traveled from city to city by train on Pullman sleeper railcars to play wherever they were invited and they took the field against whoever wanted to play them.

Opponents for these black teams included small town, white semi-professional teams. However, it was those games the black teams played against each other during the early years of the new century which gave birth to the historic legacy of African American baseball.

Many of the players on these teams were good enough to at the very least been given a chance to play in the Major Leagues. Some of them were college trained athletes while others perfected their skills playing in the military. Most of them however, developed their abilities on the baseball sandlots in black communities across the country, coming from different social and economic backgrounds with love for the game their common bond.

On these teams were such great players as "Smokey" Joe Williams, Frank Grant, Sol White, "Cannonball" Dick Redding, John Henry "Pop" Lloyd, and others. With no formal leagues, there was no set schedule of games. The players did not have contracts binding them to their teams. Many players jumped from team to team each year playing for whoever offered them the most money. This made it hard for teams to operate from year to year and many went out of business.

The Negro Leagues

Andrew "Rube" Foster addressed the need for organization in black baseball. Foster was so good as a pitcher he got the nickname "Rube" after one of the best hurlers in the Major Leagues in the early 1900s, Rube Waddell. By 1920, Foster was also the manager and owner of the Chicago American Giants. He envisioned having a league of black teams patterned after Major League baseball. On February 14, 1920 in Kansas City, Missouri, Foster initiated a meeting with other owners of black independent teams to form the Negro National League (NNL). The original NNL had eight teams: Chicago Giants, Chicago American Giants, St. Louis Giants, Detroit Stars, Indianapolis ABCs, New York Cubans, Dayton Marcos, and Kansas City Monarchs.

In 1923, another black professional baseball league was formed, the Eastern Colored League (ECL). This league originally had five teams: Brooklyn Royals Giants, Lincoln Giants of New York, Bacharach Giants of Atlantic City, Baltimore Black Sox, and the Hilldale Club of Darby, Pennsylvania.

The first Negro League World Series was held in 1924 with the Kansas City Monarchs defeating the Hilldale Club. This Series featured such talented players as Judy Johnson, Louis Santop, and Raleigh "Biz" Mackey for Hilldale and Jose Mendez, Wilber "Bullet" Rogan, and Frank Duncan for Kansas City.

Babe Ruth and the New York Yankees were the main baseball sports page headlines in the 1920s, but African Americans also had their baseball heroes: Oscar Charleston, James "Cool Papa" Bell, Martin Dihigo, and others. They all played in the Negro Leagues

The Depression Years

The 1929 stock market crash sent the United States into the worst economic depression in its history. Millions of African Americans became unemployed and did not have money to support black professional baseball. Due to financial shortcomings and internal disputes between team owners, the ECL had disbanded in 1928 prior to the crash. Andrew Foster died in December of 1930 after a lengthy illness that had kept him from being involved in the NNL. Without his leadership the league could not survive the economic storm black baseball faced and it disbanded after the 1931 season. Many black teams went out of business, but others found ways to keep operating despite their economic struggles. Two teams, the Kansas City Monarchs and Homestead Grays took to the road playing white semi-professional teams in rural small towns. The black teams that kept operating in the early 1930s launched the careers of Leroy "Satchel" Paige, Josh Gibson, Buck Leonard, and others.

To make needed extra money, many Major League players formed teams after the regular season to play exhibition games against black teams. Not surprisingly, the black teams won many of these games. The Major League players participating in those games experienced the big league caliber talent of African Americans first hand. However, black players were still kept out of the Major Leagues because the myth that they were not talented enough was perpetuated by Major League team owners.

In 1933, seven black teams came together and formed a new league, the Negro National Association of Baseball Clubs (called the Negro National League). The Pittsburgh Crawfords, Homestead Grays, Chicago American Giants, Nashville Elite Giants, Indianapolis ABCs, Detroit Stars, and Columbus Blue Birds, were the teams in the new league.

The first Negro League East West All Star Game was played that year on September 10 in Chicago's Comiskey Park. The West All Stars beat the East All Stars 11 – 7. The annual game became the national showcase for Negro League baseball. It was an African American sporting event black people would travel from all across the country to Chicago each year to see and it helped make all baseball fans more aware of black professional players.

The Negro National League continued to survive in spite of the economic depression. Each year there were some teams that went out of business, some moved to different cities, and new teams were even added. Other teams that were a part of the NNL at one time or another during the depression years were the Baltimore Elite Giants (moved from Nashville), New York Black Yankees, New York Cubans, Newark Eagles, and Philadelphia Stars.

In 1936, another league was formed, the Negro American League (NAL). The Chicago American Giants, Kansas City Monarchs, Detroit Stars, Cincinnati Tigers, St. Louis Stars, Indianapolis Athletics, Birmingham Black Barons, and Memphis Red Sox were the initial teams in the NAL.

The War Years

During America's participation in World War II (1941 – 1945), President Franklin D. Roosevelt did not cancel any of the Major League baseball seasons. He believed the national pastime was needed for Americans to have recreational diversion from the war. The Negro Leagues also continued to operate despite losing many players to military service and high paying military related factory jobs.

The economic condition of black baseball was better than the previous decade due to the improved economic status of African Americans in northern cities. America's desperate need for laborers in military production industries during the war led to job opportunities for African Americans. Black baseball as a business peaked during the war years as Negro League game attendance reached new levels.

For the first time since the 1920s, the Negro League World Series was played in this decade. The winners during the period: Homestead Grays (1943, 1944, 1948), Kansas City Monarchs (1942), Cleveland Buckeyes (1945), Newark Eagles (1946), and New York Cubans (1947).

The Final Years

The victorious end of World War II signaled the beginning of the end for the Negro Leagues. After the war, black newspapers and civil rights organizations began to seriously question Major League baseball's "whites only" policy. Was it right for African Americans to risk their lives fighting to keep America free, but then not be allowed to play the national pastime in the big leagues because of their skin color? This began the push to integrate Major League baseball because the answer to that question was "NO".

When Jackie Robinson took the field in a Brooklyn Dodger uniform on April 15, 1947 the "invisible color line" was finally broken. He became the first African American to play Major League baseball in the 20th Century. Robinson had briefly played with the

Kansas City Monarchs before signing with the Dodgers, who were in the National League. Later that summer, Larry Doby of the Newark Eagles signed with the Cleveland Indians and became the first African American to play in the American League.

It was too late for some of the best black players. Josh Gibson had died earlier that year. Buck Leonard, Oscar Charleston, and others were past their prime as ballplayers. However, it was not too late for Roy Campanella, Monte Irvin, Willie Mays, Ernie Banks, and Henry Aaron, who all first played in the Negro Leagues. They all went on to have Hall of Fame careers in the Major Leagues. The dream of young black boys to play in the Major Leagues had become a reality.

The number of teams in the Negro Leagues drastically declined as Major League teams signed more of the top African American players. Negro League game attendance dropped as black fans became more interested in Major League games due to the influx of black players. With losing their best players and their fan support, Negro League teams could no longer financially survive and Negro League baseball disappeared by the early 1960s.

PROFILES - PLAYERS

CHAPTER 2

Frank Grant

In July of 1886 the Buffalo Bisons signed a new second baseman, Frank Grant. The Buffalo Express newspaper indicated the minor league team's new player was from Spain. But Grant was no tan skinned Spaniard. He was African American. The Bisons knew having Grant on the team could create problems so they tried to pass him off as being from the European country of bullfighting and Don Quixote. African American players were not welcome in professional baseball at that time due to racial prejudice and discrimination. Despite the adverse racial attitudes against them, there were several known African American players on white teams at the highest levels of organized professional baseball during the 1880's; John W. "Bud" Fowler, Moses Fleetwood Walker, Weldy Walker, Robert Higgins, Richard Johnson, George Stovey, Sol White, Rudolph Jackson, and Ulysses F. (Frank) Grant. Not only was Frank Grant the best of this group, but also one of the best baseball players of that era.

Born on August 1, 1865 in Pittsfield, Massachusetts, Grant's family called him "Frank" after his father Franklin who died four months later. The popularity of baseball at that time was growing. It started as a game played by wealthy young men in New York City social clubs. By the beginning of the Civil War in 1861, it was no longer a "rich man's" game. During the war, baseball was played in both Union and Confederate army camps, and the love for it was spreading throughout the country as the war ended the year Frank Grant was born.

Despite New England being an area then as now more known for winter sports activity, the baseball bug reached the Western Massachusetts town of Pittsfield and bit Frank Grant. At first while growing up he was a pitcher. However, when he became a teenager he left home to be a catcher for a team in Plattsburgh, New York. By the time he was 20, Grant had found his ideal position, his "heaven" on the diamond; second base.

In the early years of professional baseball the attitude towards black and Hispanic players was grounded in racial prejudice. Both the National League formed in 1876, and the American League formed in 1901, would not allow them the opportunity to play baseball. The "color line" was drawn, but there were cracks in it that allowed Frank Grant and a few other blacks to play on white professional teams.

Grant began his professional career playing for Meriden, Connecticut in the Eastern League at a time when the game was still evolving. Batting averages were high as the batter had four strikes and a walk counted as a hit. Teams were built on speed, not power. The Meriden team broke up in July of 1886 and that's when Grant joined the Buffalo Bisons who were in the International Association, one of the top minor leagues. In his first at bat Grant hit a triple. He hit .340 for the remaining 45 games and a national sports magazine called him the best all-around player to wear a Bison uniform.

The next year Grant helped lead Buffalo to a second place finish. Not only was he the team's leading hitter at .366, but he also hit with power. Although only 5'7", 155 lbs., he was the league's leading slugger hitting 11 home runs, 27 doubles, 11 triples, and he stole 40 bases. Grant hit for the cycle (home run, triple, double, & single) in one game and stole home twice in two others. An acrobatic fielder with a strong throwing arm, he also played shortstop or third base when needed.

In spite of his success on the playing field, Grant had trouble due to the color of his skin. Fans shouted racially insulting comments from the grandstands at him, including the Bison fateful who never believed the claim he was from Spain. Grant was a target for opposing pitchers when he batted as they constantly hit him. Opposing base runners tried to hurt him on putout plays at second base. Instead of the previously customary head first slide, they started sliding feet first to cut Grant's legs with the metal spikes on their baseball shoes. When he began wearing wooden leg castings for protection, the white players sharpened their spikes in order to split the wood when their feet hit his legs.

Grant also faced opposition from his teammates. They made constant threats of physical harm and complained of having to travel with him. In 1888 they refused to sit with him for the team photo.

For a while it appeared these racial problems did not stop Frank Grant as he hit .326 in 95 games with 19 doubles, six triples, 11 home runs, and stole 26 bases in 1888. But eventually the prejudice and verbal abuse took its toll as it began to negatively affect how he played his position. Grant sometimes intentionally missed balls to prevent being purposely spiked or run over when trying to turn a double play. He was switched to play in the outfield for his protection. Finally, before the start of the 1889 season, his teammates threatened to quit if Grant played again so the Bisons didn't re-sign him.

But the racism that kept Grant and African American players out of professional baseball gave birth to a number of black independent professional baseball teams in the 1890's that made their living playing against lower level white minor league teams, other black teams, and amateur or semi-professional white teams. This was before the first official Negro professional league, the Negro National League, was formed in 1920. These black teams gave Frank Grant and other black players the opportunity to play when the doors of white professional baseball shut them out.

After being let go by the Bisons, Grant played for the Cuban Giants in 1889. Some historians say the Giants were the first African American professional baseball team. Organized in 1885, the original team consisted of black waiters from a popular summer resort on Long Island, New York; the Argyle Hotel. The baseball games were entertainment for the hotel guests. The team so quickly got the reputation for playing good baseball it was rumored they really were not waiters but hired players from black amateur teams out of Philadelphia. The name "Cuban Giants" was used in an effort to hide it being an African American team. In an attempt to keep up their masquerade, the players would try to speak Spanish while on the field. But what they spoke turned out not to be Spanish; it was an undistinguishable, strange language that puzzled spectators. In 1889 they represented the city of Trenton, New Jersey in a white professional league, the Middle States League.

The league changed its name the next year to the Eastern Interstate League and the Cuban Giants represented the city of York, Pennsylvania. They were called the York Monarchs. However, Grant and Clarence Williams were lured away by the offer of more money to play for the Harrisburg, Pennsylvania team in the same league. The Giants sued, but the court awarded both players to Harrisburg.

By midseason the Harrisburg team switched to a higher league (American Association) despite receiving protests from competitors about having African American players. To appease its detractors, the team released Williams but kept Grant. Although Grant's treatment by his Harrisburg teammates and opposing players was better than when he was with the Buffalo Bisons, he still faced racial prejudice when traveling with the team. There were hotels that refused to give him a room or wouldn't allow him to eat in their restaurant dining area with their other guests. Not signed by Harrisburg for the 1891 season, Grant discovered the doors of white professional baseball had been completely shut for African American ballplayers. He returned to the Cuban Giants. The "invisible color line" was set in stone and forced him to play for black professional teams the remainder of his baseball career.

One negative characteristic of black professional baseball evident in Grant's playing career was many of the black teams had economic problems and did not exist long before going out business. Another was African American ballplayers constantly switching from team to team for more money. There was no "reserve clause", as existed in white organized baseball, binding a player to his team the length of his contract. In some cases, African American ballplayers had no written contracts, only a verbal agreement with their team. There were too many instances of a team stealing another team's players.

One involved Grant before the 1891 season began. He along with some other Cuban Giant teammates switched over to play for the New York Big Gorhams, who had offered them more money. The Gorhams had also signed George Stovey who was considered the best African American pitcher of that era. The team is said to have had a 41 game winning streak and a record of 100 – 4 that year. When the Big Gorhams disbanded the next year, Grant and the others went back to the Cuban Giants and it became the premier black team in the eastern United States through 1895.

There are two versions of what happen to Grant and the Cuban Giants in 1897. One is the team was purchased by E. B. Lamar Jr.

and he changed its name to the Cuban X Giants. The other is Lamar forced the Cuban Giants out of business by stealing its players for his new team. Grant played with the Cuban X Giants the next two seasons as it became one of the best black teams at the turn of the century. In 1900 he was approached by a familiar face, John Bright, the former owner of the Cuban Giants. Bright lured him to captain a new team to rival the Cuban X Giants, the Genuine Cuban Giants. However, they were never able to match the success of Grant's former teams.

After the new century began, Grant was recruited by former Cuban Giants teammate Sol White to play for a newly formed team in which White had part ownership; the Philadelphia Giants. Grant helped build the foundation that made the Giants one of the strongest African American teams of the early 20th century. When Grant left the Giants in 1903 they were rivaling his former team, the Cuban X Giants, for black baseball supremacy.

Frank Grant returned to New York after the 1903 season and briefly played with a few local semi-professional teams before retiring. After baseball, he spent his years working in New York City as a waiter and a hotel porter. He died in 1937, nine years before Jackie Robinson successfully integrated white organized baseball. Grant was buried in a Clifton, New Jersey cemetery for the poor. His grave is unmarked.

But, Frank Grant is no pauper to African American baseball history. He began the path to integrate professional baseball that Jackie Robinson would successfully complete 60 years later. He crashed through baseball's "invisible color line" while it was being drawn and played three consecutive seasons at the top minor league level (1886 – 1888). Grant faced the racist wrath of his teammates, opposing players, and fans. But he overcame it to be one of the best players of that league.

And when the "invisible color line" was solidly etched in stone to keep African Americans out of professional baseball, Frank Grant played on the best professional African American teams of baseball's early period. The formation of those teams laid the foundation for what would become Negro League baseball.

Not just a good baseball player, Frank Grant was a black pioneer of America's national pastime and his election into the National Baseball Hall of Fame in 2006 cemented that fact.

CHAPTER 3

Pete Hill

A star in Negro League baseball during the first quarter of the 20th Century, Pete Hill was called the "black" Ty Cobb. Major League owners and executives futilely denied that it was not racism that kept African Americans like Hill and others out of white organized baseball during that time. This implied that black players did not have the skills and abilities for big league baseball, which was not true and why the "color line" that kept black players out was invisible. If it were true, Negro League players would not have been compared to the Major League ones as they commonly were before the "color line" was erased. John Henry "Pop" Lloyd, one of the best pre-1920 players in Negro League baseball, was referred to as the "black" Honus Wagner; his contemporary at shortstop that played for the Pittsburgh Pirates (1900 – 1917)and was inducted into the Baseball Hall of Fame in 1939. Pete Hill's accomplishments on the field were compared to Ty Cobb; who in his Major League career (1905 - 1928) hit over .400 three times, finished with a .366 career batting average, and was also inducted into the Baseball Hall of Fame in 1939. It is a comparison painted by racism, but it gives an indication of Hill's talents as a ballplayer. As Cobb was making life miserable for opposing American League pitchers, Pete Hill was the hitting superstar on three pre-1920 era premier African American teams.

At 6" 1", 215 lbs., Hill was a left handed line drive hitter that was hard to defend because he hit the ball to all fields. A contact hitter that seldom swung and missed, he was a "tough out" for right handed and left handed pitchers. Cum Posey, the long-time owner of Negro League baseball's Homestead Grays called Pete Hill, "the most consistent hitter of his time." Negro League first baseman Ben Taylor who played on teams that were opponents of Hill called him "one of the most dangerous hitters a pitcher could ever face in a tough situation." A 1910 article in the African American Chicago Defender newspaper stated, "Pete Hill would be a star in the Major Leagues if he were white. He can do anything a white player can do. He can hit, run, throw, and is what can be termed a wise, heady ballplayer".

Success in baseball is measured by statistics. For a team it is measured mainly by games won, league standing, and championships won. For players who are not pitchers it is measured by batting average, home runs, hits, runs batted in (RBI), and championships won. Collecting historical team and individual player statistics of the Negro League baseball era has been difficult due to the failure of the black leagues to keep documented official game summaries, the inconsistent coverage of Negro League games by black newspapers, and the blatant ignoring of black baseball by major white newspapers. Despite the difficulties, historical data has been researched to paint a partial statistical picture for Negro League stars like Pete Hill. And then there are the stories, both true and exaggerated, that make up Negro League baseball folklore that add to their picture.

The statistical and historical portrait of Pete Hill is one of being a hitting machine throughout his entire baseball career. Hill ended a season hitting over .300 eight times, over .400 twice. He had hitting streaks of 27 games in 1910 and 14 games in 1912. Twenty-nine times he got four or more hits in a game. In 1904, Hill had a six hit game and three games when he had five hits. The next year there were twenty games in which he stroked three hits. He also hit with power: six times clubbing two or more home runs in a game during his career.

But Pete Hill could do more than hit. A superb defensive centerfielder with a strong, accurate throwing arm he also had speed running the bases that caused havoc for opponents.

Pittsburgh, Pennsylvania has a rich baseball tradition. The Pittsburgh Pirates have been a part of Major League Baseball since 1900, winning five World Series Championships (1909, 1925, 1960, 1971, and 1979). Players on the Pirates during those early years included Honus Wagner, Paul Waner, and Pie Traynor; all in baseball's Hall of Fame.

A part of Pittsburgh's baseball tradition is the role the city has in the history of African American baseball. The Pittsburgh Keystones were one of the many African American teams born around 1900 when racism began keeping black players out of professional baseball. Pittsburgh was also the original home for the Pittsburgh Crawfords and Homestead Grays. The 1931 Grays and the 1932 Crawfords both get votes for the best Negro League team ever assembled. Satchel Paige, Oscar Charleston, Buck Leonard, "Cool Papa" Bell, and Josh Gibson are just a few of the Negro League great players that wore a Pittsburgh team uniform at one time during their careers.

Because the baseball career of Pete Hill also began in Pittsburgh, as a teenager with the Pittsburgh Keystones in 1899, it was initially assumed he was from the former "steel city". However, additional research on his life resulted in changes to his biographical information. His legal name was John Preston Hill, not Joseph as what was previously written. Also, it appears he was born in Virginia (Culpeper County) around 1882 - 1884. It is not known when he moved to Pittsburgh, but it is a very high probability that is where Hill learned to play the game.

In 1901, Hill left Pittsburgh for New York to play for the Cuban X Giants. Being only 21, he could not break into the starting lineup to play regularly. But, the young outfielder caught the eye of Sol White, manager of the X Giants' main rival, the Philadelphia Giants. White recruited Hill to play for his team in 1903.

With the Philadelphia Giants, he began to mature as a ballplayer. In 1904, he was the centerfielder for what many say was the best black team of the early 20th century era. With Hill leading the way, the Giants were proclaimed winners of the "Colored Championship of the World" in 1904, 1905, and 1906. This was the title given to the top black team on the east coast. Charles "Kid" Carter, James Booker, Charlie Grant, Emmett Bowman, and Dan McClellan were other good players on the Giants with Hill.

Another teammate of Hill was Andrew "Rube" Foster. Foster at that time was one of the best pitchers in black baseball. He would later become the "father" of Negro League baseball and a member of the Baseball Hall of Fame. The friendship with Foster would have a major influence on the remainder of Pete Hill's baseball career.

After the 1906 season, Foster left the Philadelphia Giants to become the manager for the Chicago Leland Giants. He took six of his Philadelphia Giants teammates with him, including Pete Hill.

Under the leadership of Rube Foster, Hill's career blossomed with the Chicago team. He was the team captain and was taught the ins and outs of managing by his friend. Hill continued to build on his reputation as a great hitter and the Leland Giants became one of the most dominant African American teams in the country's heartland.

Although undocumented, it is said the 1910 team won over 120 games. Along with Hill, the team included good players such as "Pop" Lloyd, Bruce Petway and Grant "Home Run" Johnson. Hill was the team's leading hitter batting .428.

Wanting more control over the team, Foster got into a disagreement with the owner of the Giants Frank Leland after the 1910 season. When he resigned and started his own team, the Chicago American Giants, Foster took with him the best players from the Leland Giants, which included his friend and team captain Pete Hill. The American Giants quickly became well known throughout the country. The team was almost as popular as the Chicago White Sox and the Chicago Cubs. One Sunday in 1911 the American Giants drew more fans than both of the Chicago Major League teams.

When given the chance throughout his career, Pete Hill proved he could hit Major League pitching. Despite being kept out of white organized professional baseball, African American ballplayers had the opportunity to compete against white professional players. In the fall after the regular season ended, many white players would make extra money by forming teams to play exhibition games against Negro League players. This practice was called "barnstorming" as the white and black teams would travel from city to city to play the games. Because the black teams would win as many or even more times than the white ones, Major League executives unsuccessfully tried to discourage their players from barnstorming. Black players also competed against white Major Leaguers in the winter leagues that operated during November and December in the Caribbean and California.

While with the Philadelphia Giants in 1906, Pete Hill batted .428 in exhibition games against the American League's Philadelphia Athletics with Hall of Fame pitchers Rube Waddell and Eddie Plank. In 1910 with the Chicago Leland Giants, Hill batted .350 in an exhibition series against a Major League All- Star team.

Hill played in the Cuban Winter League where Major Leaguers, African American players, and the best Latin American players competed on the same field. Black players loved playing in Cuba because they didn't face the racism that confronted them in the United States. In the 1910 Cuban Winter League season, Hill batted .300 in 11 games against Major League pitching. That same year in Cuba, he also played against the Detroit Tigers who had finished 3rd in the American League. Hill batted .273 in those games. He batted .318 against Major League pitchers in two other Cuban Winter League seasons.

Major League executive refused to look at the performances of African American players in these exhibition and winter league games as an indication of Major League potential. Claiming the white players did not compete in those contests with the same intensity as a regular season game, the executives ignored the results. However, to Hill and other Negro League players, it confirmed what they already had known. If they were given the opportunity they could make it in the Major Leagues; a fact the white players they competed against also realized.

In 1919 the heavily favored Chicago White Sox were upset in the World Series by the Cincinnati Redlegs. However, before the next season began eight of the White Sox players were on trial for accepting money from gamblers to lose the Series. While Major League Baseball was trying to handle the fallout from that scandal, a new era was beginning in Negro League baseball; and Pete Hill was a part of it.

Rube Foster became co-owner of another team in 1919, the Detroit Stars, and named Hill as the team's manager. The Stars would be a part of a new league Foster organized in 1920, the Negro National League (NNL). The first organized official Negro professional baseball league, the NNL had eight teams; the Chicago American Giants, Chicago Giants, Indianapolis ABCs, Kansas City Monarchs, St. Louis Giants, Cuban Stars (Cincinnati), Columbus Buckeyes, and Detroit Stars. Hill used what he learned from Foster to lead the team as manager and as a player he led the team with his bat. Even though he was 38 years old, Hill batted .368 in 1919. The next year he batted .275 and the Stars tied for second place in the initial season for the NNL. Then although he was 40 years old, Hill batted over .300 for the Stars in 1921.

Going back to the east coast, Pete Hill played with the Philadelphia Royal Giants in 1922. But his old friend Rube Foster called again and Hill in 1923 became the player/manager of the Milwaukee Bears, a new team co-owned by Foster in the NNL. Hill only played part time, but he still had his batting stroke at age 42 as he hit .296.

The final days of Pete Hill's baseball career were with the Baltimore Black Sox beginning in 1924. The Black Sox were in the Eastern Colored League (ECL), the second official Negro professional baseball league formed a year earlier. He was their player/manager for two years, playing his last game in 1925.

After baseball, Hill worked for the Ford Motor Company in Detroit. He died on December 19, 1951 in Buffalo, New York. Even in death Hill's ties to Chicago through his friend Rube Foster remained evident. He was buried in the Holy Sepulchre Cemetery in Alsip, Illinois, a town within the metropolitan Chicago area. Recently through the efforts of Negro League historians, the unmarked grave sites of many former Negro League players are being discovered and provided with a grave or headstone. Hill's unmarked site in the Alsip cemetery has been found recently and a gravestone is planned for it.

Although his best years as a player were before the 1920s, Pete Hill was not unknown to those who followed African American baseball. A poll taken in the early 1950s by the Pittsburgh Courier, an African American newspaper, of black baseball fans voted him the fourth best outfielder in Negro League history. Only Oscar Charleston, Monte Irvin, and Cristobal Torriente received more votes. They were the only ones able to attain the high standard of excellence for outfielders set by Hill before their Negro League baseball careers began.

With his induction into baseball's Hall of Fame in 2006, Pete Hill will now become more known to all who love the game. Even though he was not allowed to play in the Major Leagues, Hill played the game in a way that can't be ignored. His name deserves to be mentioned along with Ty Cobb and Tris Speaker (Baseball Hall of Fame 1937) in any conversation about the greatest outfielders of baseball's pre-1920 period.

CHAPTER 4

Jose Mendez

Hall of Fame player John Henry Lloyd faced many excellent pitchers during his Negro League baseball career. Lloyd batted against "Smokey" Joe Williams and Andrew "Rube" Foster, both of which are also in the Hall of Fame; and he faced "Cannonball" Dick Redding one of the hardest throwing pitchers (black or white) prior to 1920. But Lloyd said of all the great hurlers he faced, "There were none better than Jose Mendez."

A national hero in his homeland of Cuba, Mendez was called by his fellow Cubans "El Diamante"; The Black Diamond. A few light-skinned Cubans were able to step across the color line to play in the Major Leagues during the early 20th Century, but Mendez was dark-skinned, a Cuban of African descent. Not able to look like a white player, Mendez played in the Negro Leagues and became the first Hispanic baseball legend in America.

Jose de la Caridad Mendez was born March 19, 1887 in the Cuban province of Matanzas, a major sugar production area. But the Mendez family was not involved in sugar cane farming, they were craftsmen. Jose was trained as a carpenter. Matanzas was also known for African flavored Cuban music as demonstrated by Jose's talent at playing the clarinet and the guitar.

Baseball was also important in Matanzas. Many Cuban's believe the province is the birthplace of Cuban baseball, where the first baseball game was played in the nation (December 27, 1874). Although historical evidence has shown this not to be true, it added to Mendez's aura as coming from the baseball hallowed grounds of Matanzas.

At 5'8" and weighing 155 pounds, Mendez was smaller than the other good pitchers of his era. "Smokey" Joe Williams was 6'4". The best pitcher in the Major Leagues at that time, Walter "Big Train" Johnson was 6'1". But his size was Mendez's deceptive ally against batters. He had long fingers that allowed him to have exceptional spin on his pitches. With his long arms and rangy body, Mendez gave hitters a slow and easy pitching motion. But he threw blazing fastballs that did not move in a straight line and sharp snapping curveballs, pitches not expected from someone of his slight built. Negro League umpire Bert Gholston described Mendez as a "wily pitcher with lionhearted courage".

Mendez made his American debut in 1908 with the Cuban Stars, a team of players from Cuba and other Latin American countries that played mainly against African American teams. Although he pitched briefly for the Brooklyn Royal Giants that same summer, Mendez established his pitching prowess in the United States with the Stars.

He became a national hero in Cuba that fall in a series of exhibition games against the Cincinnati Reds in Havana. Pitching for the Cuban League's Almendares team, Mendez hurled 25 consecutive scoreless innings against the Reds. He threw a one hit shutout his first appearance, seven scoreless innings of relief the next one, and another shutout the final game. In the three games, Mendez struck out 24 Cincinnati batters. This is considered as one of the greatest achievements in Cuban baseball history. Cuba was not an independent country at that time as it was under military occupation due to the United States' victory in the Spanish-American War (1898). Cubans saw Mendez's pitching dominance of the Reds as not just a win on the baseball field, but as a victory over their military conqueror.

From 1909-1914, Mendez was a fearsome pitcher in both the United States and Cuba. With the Cuban Stars in 1909, he was 14 -2 which included pitching a 10 inning no-hitter. One of the losses was to Rube Foster and the Chicago American Giants. Mendez matched the great Foster pitch for pitch before losing 1-0. One of Mendez's teammates dropped a fly ball that allowed the Giants to score an unearned run. Against the New York Lincoln Giants in 1911, Mendez and "Smokey Joe" Williams tangled in a nine inning, scoreless pitching duel. Williams gave up no hits, Mendez only two. The Stars won the game in extra innings. During his years in the Cuban Winter League, Mendez posted a 53 -17 record which included success against Major League teams. He defeated both Hall of Fame pitching stars Christy Mathewson (New York Giants) and Eddie Plank (Philadelphia Phillies) twice. Giants' manager John McGraw said, "Mendez would be worth $50,000 if he pitched in the Major Leagues". But McGraw made no effort to sign Mendez and challenge Major League Baseball's "invisible color line".

The career of "El Diamante Negro" made a drastic change after the 1914 season when at age 27 severe soreness developed in his pitching arm. Faced with the possibility of not pitching again, Mendez proved he was more than just a good pitcher. Leaving the Cuban Stars, he joined a team called All Nations as a shortstop. Formed in 1912 by James Leslie Wilkinson who would later be the owner of the Kansas City Monarchs, All Nations was a barnstorming team that traveled using its own custom made railroad car. The players on the team were of all races and nationalities: African American, white, Hispanic, Indians, Asian, etc.

After three years with All Nations, Mendez played shortstop and outfield for the Chicago American Giants in 1918 and the Detroit Stars in 1919. However, his pitching arm continued to be sore. When the first Negro professional baseball league, the Negro National League (NNL), was formed in 1920, League President Rube Foster made an effort to have a balanced distribution of talent between the new league's teams. He took Mendez from the Detroit Stars and assigned him to J. L. Wilkinson's Kansas City Monarchs. Owning the All Nations team Mendez had played with earlier, Wilkinson named Jose as the Monarch's player/manager.

Under Mendez, the Monarchs won the Negro National League pennants from 1923-1925. He managed the team with a soft spoken, fair, but tough approach that got the attention and respect of his players. Mendez also began to pitch again. Although he was not the "El Diamante Negro" of his earlier years, he was still an effective pitcher having a 12 - 4 record in 1923.

After a second Negro professional baseball league was formed in 1923, the Eastern Colored League (ECL), the first Negro League World Series took place the following year. The 1924 Series pitted the Hilldale Club of Darby, Pennsylvania (a town located within the metropolitan Philadelphia area) of the Eastern Colored League against the Negro National League's Kansas City Monarchs, managed by Jose Mendez. It showcased some of the best African American players of that era. Along with Mendez on the Monarchs were Hall of Fame pitcher Wilber "Bullet" Rogan, William Drake, and Newt Allen. The Hilldale Club had Louis Santop, William "Judy" Johnson, and Raleigh "Biz" Mackey, all now with plaques in Cooperstown. The Series was a best five out of nine contests and was played not only in Philadelphia and Kansas City, but also Baltimore and Chicago to allow more African American fans to see it.

Tied at four games apiece, the Series came down to the last deciding winner take all game. The Monarchs had used their best pitchers the previous two games and there was a question as to who would pitch the most important game of the year. When Monarchs owner J. L. Wilkinson posed that question to Mendez, he was surprised Mendez replied; "Jose Mendez." After having surgery on his arm earlier in the year, doctors had advised Mendez not to pitch that season. But he had already pitched 10 innings in relief the previous games in the Series and he felt the Monarchs' best chance of winning was with him on the mound. He was right. At 36 years old, Mendez no longer had the blazing fast ball of his youth. However, he had perfect control of his curveball and change of pace pitches that kept the Hilldale hitters off balanced and confused, surrendering only three hits. The Monarchs won 2-0 and were the first Negro League World Series champions.

The Monarchs and Hilldale met in the Negro World Series the following year with the outcome being different, Hilldale won 5 games to 1. Mendez lost Game 3 of the Series, 3-1.

After managing the Monarchs in 1926, Mendez retired to Cuba. But he continued to pitch. He won his last game on January 21, 1927. Shortly thereafter, he was diagnosed with tuberculosis and died in 1928. He was 41 years old.

There have been many accolades to Joes Mendez's baseball abilities. He was one of the first players inducted into the Cuban

Baseball Hall of Fame in 1939. He along with Martin Dihigo and Cristobal Torriente are acknowledged as to have been the top Hispanic players in Negro League baseball. And Mendez's induction into the National Baseball Hall of Fame in 2006 cemented his place in America's baseball history.

In response to his death in 1928, there were also words of tribute to Jose Mendez the man, to his character. Former teammates, opponents, and players he managed spoke of his intelligence, courage, and grace. They described him as a well-spoken, humble man who despite his tremendous ability was not full of pride and ego. He did not engage in loud and vulgar self-promotion. He let his pitching do his talking. All agreed that Jose Mendez, the baseball player and the man, had class.

CHAPTER 5

Louis Santop

The number of home runs Louis Santop hit during his career in Negro League baseball (1910 – 1926) is not known. Negro League statistics were not kept consistently from year to year and box scores for many of the games were not recorded or have been lost. But what is known about Santop is he could hit a baseball a long way. The distances of his home runs are legendary Negro League lore. Stories are told of the great Josh Gibson's home runs that got him the nickname "the black Babe Ruth" in the 1930's. But Louis Santop was the first African American player to hit the baseball for such great distances that in the early 1920's black fans compared him to the "Great Bambino", Babe Ruth.

At 6'4", 240 lbs., Louis Santop was a true slugger. He hit 500 and 400 feet home runs during an era when the ball was not designed to travel such distances, the "dead ball" era (1900 – 1919). The baseball's center core during that time was not tightly wound making it softer and more difficult to hit very far. But, Santop was strong enough to hit home runs that were legendary due to the distances they traveled. Because the ball seemed to launch off his bat, he was nicknamed "Big Bertha" after the German's World War I long range artillery pieces. The left handed batting catcher could also hit for a high average. Although not fully verified, "Big Bertha" hit over .400 many times.

Santop could not only hit, he was an excellent catcher with a strong throwing arm. As a part of baseball game strategy, the pitcher works with the catcher to silence the bats of the opponent. A pitcher has to have confidence in his catcher to be effective. Two of the best pitchers in Negro League baseball had such confidence in Louis Santop. During his career, he was the battery mate for both "Smokey" Joe Williams who was inducted in the National Baseball Hall of Fame in 1999 and "Cannonball" Dick Redding. By the time the first official league was formed in 1920, "Big Bertha" was established as one of the first African American baseball superstars.

The state of Texas bred and developed many Negro League players. Rube Foster from Winchester, Willie Foster from Calvert, Willie Wells from Austin, Biz Mackey from Eagle Pass, and Hilton Smith from Lincoln (10 miles north of Giddings) were just a few of them from the Lone Star State. Born on January 17, 1890 in Tyler as Louis Santop Lofton, "Big Bertha" was a part of the Texas fraternity. The "Lofton" was dropped from his name by the time he was nineteen and burst unto the African American professional baseball scene.

To play wherever and whenever they could to make money was the typical lifestyle of an African American baseball player in the beginning of the Twentieth Century. In 1909 Santop began the season playing for one of the many black semi-pro teams in Texas, the Fort Worth Wonders. However, as the season progressed, he was with another black semi-pro team, the Monarchs of Guthrie, Oklahoma.

It was a testament to Santop's baseball talent that the big, strong catcher playing in small town Oklahoma would come to the attention of Sol White, manager/co-owner of the Philadelphia Giants. Although no official Negro League existed in 1909, most of the top black baseball teams were on the east coast. White's Philadelphia Giants were one of those top teams, considered by many the best black professional baseball team of the early Twentieth Century. It was a whirlwind season for Santop, a nineteen year old kid from east Texas, starting in Fort Worth and ending with him playing in Philadelphia.

Due to a dispute with his business partner, Sol White left the Philadelphia Giants in 1911 and became the manager of a new African American team formed in New York City's Harlem area, the New York Lincoln Giants. Because there were few if any African American teams with enforceable written contracts with players, White was able to take Santop with him to New York. It was with the Lincoln Giants that Santop's career began to flourish. The team was stocked with such good players as Hall of Famer John Henry Lloyd, Grant Johnson, and Spottswood Poles. Also, on the Lincoln Giants with Santop were pitchers "Smokey Joe" Williams, a fellow Texan from Seguin, and former Philadelphia Giants teammate "Cannonball" Dick Redding. As a catcher Santop was outstanding as he handled both Williams and Redding, two of the hardest throwing pitchers in baseball at that time. But it was as a hitter that "Big Bertha" began to create his legacy. From 1911 – 1914 although not verified, it is said he hit .400 each year. And then there were the demonstrations of his strength, according to legend, as he hit a 500 foot home run and several over 450 feet while a Lincoln Giant.

It was with the Lincoln Giants that Santop became a crowd pleaser. In adding to the fans' game attendance experience, Negro League players would sometime put on exhibitions prior to the game for entertainment. It was not clowning or acting according to the negative stereotypical picture painted of African Americans at that time of being shiftless and lazy. Not taking away from the serious nature of the proceeding contest, the players would put their baseball talents on display during pre-game warm up. Standing at home plate, Santop would throw the ball over the centerfield fence (400+ feet) and then while in his catcher's squat quickly fire the ball with straight line accuracy to the infielder at each base (first, second, and third) for fifteen minutes. During batting practice, he would amaze the crowd by the distances he hit the ball.

Living in New York did not take the Texas out of Santop. He rolled his own cigarettes, a custom he learned back home. Having a "Texas" tough competitive spirit, when necessary he ignored injury to play. Santop once caught a doubleheader with a broken thumb and got the key hits to win both games. Unlike what would be expected of someone of his large physical stature, he did not purposely intimidate other players. Santop kept his East Texas good natured, amiable attitude. However, when riled he could show his strength. Negro League great Oscar Charleston discovered this when he received three broken ribs due to a Santop bear hug during an altercation.

The Lincoln Giants were the most dominant team in African American baseball from 1911 – 1913. However, in 1914 while the team was going through an ownership dispute, Santop was lured away by Rube Foster to join the Chicago American Giants. But Santop's ties to New York were too strong. The former Lincoln Giants formed a new team, the Lincoln Stars, and was able to get Santop and most of the former Giants' players back by season's end. Quickly the Stars became one of the most dominant teams in the

East through the middle of the 1917 season and then it was disbanded.

In the fall of 1917 before he served in the Navy, Santop was recruited by Hilldale to play in a series of exhibition games against a team of Major League players. The Hilldale team was out of the Philadelphia suburb of Darby. Starting as an athletic organization for boys in 1910, the Hilldale Athletic Club, it had grown into a professional level baseball organization under the direction of owner Ed Bolden. Some eyewitness accounts say the Hilldale team won two out of the three games played and Santop had six hits during the series.

After missing the 1918 and 1919 seasons due to his time in the military, Santop returned to play with Hilldale. He was 30 years old and became one of the highest paid professional African American baseball players earning $500 a month. With the addition of Santop, Hilldale developed into a dominant team and in 1923 became a charter member of the Eastern Colored League (ECL), the second official Negro League baseball league. Hall of Famer Judy Johnson, Frank Warfield, and Jake Stephens were a few of Santop's notable teammates as Hilldale won the first three ECL pennants (1923 – 1925).

In 1924 the first Negro League World Series pitted Hilldale against the Kansas City Monarchs, pennant winners of the Negro National League (NNL). The Monarchs had Hall of Famer and Cuban national hero Jose Mendez as their player/manager. Also, Hall of Famer Wilber "Bullet" Rogan, Frank Duncan, and Newt Allen were on the Monarchs. League officials decided the series would be a best-of-nine game format. The first team to win five games would be champion. To maximize attendance and allow more African Americans outside of Kansas City and Philadelphia to see the series, the games would also be played in Chicago and Baltimore.

Supposedly a national showcase for Negro League baseball, the

Series became the event that tarnished Santop's brilliant career. Tied at three games apiece, Hilldale was leading in the seventh game 3 – 2 going into the bottom of the ninth inning. The Monarchs rallied to have the bases loaded, but with two outs. Hilldale was one out away from going ahead in the Series four games to two. The Monarchs batter, Frank Duncan, hit a foul fly ball behind home plate within the reach of Santop. All the normally sure handed backstop had to do was catch it and Hilldale would win. He dropped the ball! Given another swing, Duncan hit a ground ball that got through third baseman Biz Mackey driving in two runs to give Kansas City a 4 – 3 victory.

As he left the field, Santop was verbally attacked by his manager Frank Warfield for committing the error. Although Mackey should have handled Duncan's ground ball, Warfield believed Santop's error cost Hilldale the game. In front of other teammates and fans, Warfield gave his catcher a vicious, profanity filled tongue lashing. Devastated, Santop was brought to tears. Hilldale recovered to win the next game to tie the Series at four games each. But, the Monarchs won the winner take all ninth game behind the brilliant pitching of Jose Mendez to become the first Negro League World Series Champion.

Although Santop's hitting helped Hilldale win four games in the Series, all he accomplished was overshadowed by the costly error in Game Seven. Despite how well he had played the previous years, the team lost confidence in him. Mackey, who was younger, replaced him as Hilldale's number one catcher the next year. Clashing with the Monarchs again in the 1925 Negro League World Series, Hilldale got a measure of revenge winning in six games. With Mackey being the team's hitting star in the Series, Santop played very little, appearing a few times as a pinch hitter.

Released by Hilldale in the middle of the 1926 season, the thirty-six year old Santop never again played for a top team. Among Negro

League baseball players and executives, the talk was about "Big Bertha' not mentally recovering from his 1924 Negro League World Series miscue and how quickly his playing skill's eroded as he had gotten older. In less than two years he went from a superstar to fading from the Negro League baseball scene.

Remaining in Philadelphia, Santop at first became a radio broadcaster before eventually settling in for years as a bartender. On January 6, 1942, "Big Bertha" died in a Philadelphia Naval Hospital after years of debilitating illnesses, including severe arthritis, the result of his many years in baseball as a catcher.

Compared against Louis Santop's entire overall career body of work, his costly error in the 1924 Negro League World Series is just a slight blemish. His 2006 induction into the National Baseball Hall of Fame indicated his star continues to shine brightly as the first great home run slugger in Negro League baseball.

CHAPTER 6

Ben Taylor

In 1933 a young Buck Leonard was the hitting star for a black semi-pro team in Portsmouth, Virginia, the Berkley Black Sox. That June, the Baltimore Stars, a black professional traveling team came to Portsmouth to play the Black Sox. Leonard's younger brother Charlie played for the Stars. Ben Taylor, the Stars' manager, had heard that Charlie Leonard's brother was a good baseball player.

After seeing the older Leonard sibling that day, Taylor signed him to play with the Stars.

Buck Leonard first played right field, but soon Ben Taylor switched him to play first base. Taylor had been the team's first baseman, but was 45 years old and knew it was time for someone younger to take over. He taught Leonard all the ins and outs, all the fundamentals about playing the position. Under Taylor's teaching, Leonard began to become a solid, sure handed, sure footed first baseman.

Before the end of the season the Stars broke up because of financial problems and Buck Leonard went to play for the Brooklyn Royal Giants. The next season he was with the Homestead Grays and began the career in which he would become what many consider the best first baseman in Negro League baseball history. A career that would get Leonard inducted into the National Baseball Hall of Fame in 1972. A career, Leonard never hesitated to say, greatly influenced by Ben Taylor. Leonard acknowledged, "I got most of my learning from Ben Taylor. He helped me when I first broke in with his team. He had been the best first baseman in Negro baseball up until that time, and he was the one who taught me to play first base".

It is no surprise Buck Leonard turned into a good first baseman considering he had the ideal teacher in Benjamin Harrison Taylor, a smooth, sure handed fielder that teammates called "Old Reliable". Taylor made the difficult plays at first base look easy and saved his infielders from making errors by his ability to dig out of the dirt their low throws.

But, Taylor was not just a good fielder; he was a left-handed, line drive hitter that hammered the ball to all fields. Batters have weaknesses that a pitcher will try to exploit. Some have trouble hitting a curveball, some cannot handle low outside pitches, or pitches close inside. But it was said Ben Taylor had no weakness as a batter and consistently hit over .300.

Born on July 1, 1888 in Anderson, South Carolina, Taylor grew up in a home as one of thirteen children strictly ruled by his father, an African Methodist minister. Ben was the youngest of the Taylor boys that got involved in the not so religious profession of professional baseball. The oldest, Charles Isham (CI) Taylor, became one of the best managers in Negro League baseball history. "Candy" Jim Taylor was a good fielding third baseman and also became a manager, while "Steel Arm" Johnny Taylor was a pitcher. The close ties Ben had with his brothers influenced him throughout his entire Negro League career.

In 1908, Ben began first as a pitcher with the Birmingham Giants. The Giants, managed by Ben's brother CI, were one of the first black professional baseball teams in Birmingham. The other Taylor brothers, "Candy" Jim and "Steel Arm" Johnny, also played for the team. While Ben showed promise as a left handed hurler, he also began developing into a good first baseman that could hit the baseball as the Giants became one of the best black teams in the south.

CI Taylor's Negro baseball managing odyssey took him from Birmingham in 1910 to West Baden Springs, a small town in southern Indiana located near springs of mineral water. He became the manager of the West Baden Sprudels, a team sponsored by the town's large resort facility, the West Baden Springs Hotel. Although located in a remote area, the Sprudels were one of the many black independent affiliation teams in the country's heartland that existed prior to the Negro National League (NNL) being formed in 1920. Younger brothers "Steel Arm" Johnny and Ben went along with CI to Indiana.

In a dispute over money or some other undetermined reason, after one season the two younger Taylor brothers stepped from under the guiding hands of CI for the first time and played with the St. Louis Giants. They were also joined by their brother Jim. Like most sibling relationships, the one between the Taylor brothers was not perfect, but enduring. The family ties were very strong at most times, weaker at others, but stayed intact throughout the brothers' Negro League careers. This was especially true for younger brother Ben who during the early stages of his career had one, two, or all three of his brothers with him on a team. Facing a higher level of competition than he had faced before, Ben continued his development as a pitcher and first baseman with St. Louis. Although there are no records for verification, he is credited with a 30 – 1 pitching record that year.

Taylor finished the 1912 season playing for the New York Lincoln Giants. Hall of Famers John "Pop" Lloyd, Louis Santop, and "Smokey" Joe Williams were all wearing Lincoln Giant uniforms that year. There is also some research showing Ben's brother Johnny was on the team. This is an example of how a lack of records or more verifiable information can make the history of Negro League players during Ben Taylor's time unclear. It could be the Taylor on the Lincoln Giants that year was only Ben, or only Johnny, or both. Considered the top black team in the east, the Lincoln Giants played an exhibition series against the team considered the best from the Midwest; Rube Foster's Chicago American Giants. If the Lincoln Giants did add Ben Taylor late in the season, it may have been under a different name (a "ringer") to help bolster its pitching staff going into the series as there is no indication of him playing first base. In fact, since "Candy" Jim played third base for Chicago, all three Taylor brothers could have participated in the series. The Lincoln Giants won the unofficial "colored championship" defeating the Giants three games to one.

The 1913 season proved to be a turning point in the baseball career of Ben Taylor. Chicago's manager/owner Rube Foster recruited him solely to play first base. Foster was still pitching for his American Giants along with Bill Lindsey, Bill Gatewood, and others; which gave them a strong pitching staff. The addition of Taylor to go along with existing American Giants' Bingo DeMoss, Bruce Petway, and Hall of Famer Pete Hill strengthened the team. Foster had also recruited "Steel Arm" Johnny once again bringing all three Taylor brothers together on the same team.

However, the Taylor family ties tightened the next year. In 1914, CI Taylor became half owner of the Indianapolis ABCs, originally organized by the American Brewing Company. Always having a good eye for young talent, CI discovered an 18 year Indianapolis kid to play centerfield who would be a Hall of Famer; Oscar Charleston. He also stocked the ABCs with established players such as Bingo

DeMoss, David Malarcher, George Shively, and Dizzy Dismukes. In addition, CI brought all three of his younger brothers to play for his team but not just because they were family. CI Taylor was a serious minded manager who ruled his team with strict discipline. He wanted to win games and he knew his brothers could help. "Candy Jim" was an excellent defensive third baseman and "Steel Arm" Johnny was a solid pitcher. And then there was the youngest brother Ben, an excellent defensive first baseman and the ideal cleanup hitter for CI's team.

It did not take long for the ABCs to rival Rube Foster's Chicago American Giants for black baseball supremacy in America's heartland. It was the "dead ball" era. The center core of the baseball was soft, not tightly wound, making it hard for batters to hit for distance. Not many home runs were hit, resulting in teams using strategies that involved bunting, stealing bases, hitting behind the runners, and using the hit and run to score runs. Both Foster and CI Taylor were masters at using those strategies with their teams. There was also friction between the two teams as Foster was upset about losing the Taylor brothers, especially Ben, to the ABCs.

In 1916, the teams played a hotly contested exhibition series at the end of the season. In a dispute over a decision by an umpire, Foster pulled his team off the field in one game. The ABCs won the most games and it is said, but no box scores have been found documenting it, Ben Taylor hit over .600 and stole five bases in the series.

While playing with the ABCs from 1914 – 1922, Ben Taylor established himself as the best first baseman in the Negro Leagues. He still pitched occasionally, but his reputation was made at first baseman. Although not acknowledged by the white newspaper media, he was at the very least an equal contemporary with George Sisler, Frank Chance, and the other Major League first basemen of that era.

In one of those nine years Taylor left the ABCs for reasons that are unclear and conflicting. Some information says he aspired to follow in his brother CI's managerial footsteps and left to manage the New York Bacharach Giants. However, other records show

Taylor on the team in New York; but "Pop" Lloyd as the Giants' manager. Also, some records show Taylor playing for Hilldale in 1919.

For whatever reason the Taylor family ties loosened, they tightened the next year as he returned to the ABCs and the team became a charter member in the Negro National League (NNL). Ben continued his hot hitting in the new league, hitting an unverified .323 and .407 the first two years.

After the 1921 season ended, CI Taylor died unexpectedly at 47 years old. His widow, Oliva, was then the team's owner. She turned to her brother-in-law Ben for help and he became the ABCs player/manager. Along with Oscar Charleston and a young, developing catcher named Biz Mackey, Ben led the team to a second place finish in 1922.

But the ABCs were not the same to Ben without CI. Looking for a fresh start, he went back east in 1923 to organize a new team, the Washington Potomacs. He hired his brother Johnny as the team's pitching coach. The Potomacs became part of the new Eastern Colored League (ECL) the next year. Like his brother CI, Ben was a serious, by the book baseball manager; a strict disciplinarian. However, the Potomacs struggled, finishing next to last in 1924, and the team shut down due to financial problems. Although past his prime as a player, Taylor signed on with the Harrisburg Giants in 1925. Managed by former ABC teammate Oscar Charleston, the team finished second in the ECL.

In 1926 he got another opportunity to fulfill his desire to manage when he was hired by the Baltimore Black Sox. As a part of the ECL, the Black Sox were a troubled team that Taylor tried to instill discipline. He traded uncooperative players, but was not around to see the fruit of his efforts. In a trade of managers, he was sent to the Bacharach Giants in exchange for former teammate Dick Lundy before the 1929 season. With Lundy as their manager, the team won the pennant of the short lived American Negro League in 1929.

As the new decade (1930s) began, Ben Taylor continued to manage and coach with teams at lower levels of Negro League baseball competition. With each team he displayed his easygoing temperament, same as brother CI. He was also an excellent teacher of young players as exhibited with a young Buck Leonard in 1933. But Buck learned more than how to play first base from "Old Reliable". He picked up Taylor's modest and professional approach to the game. Buck developed a reputation as a gentleman during his playing career just as Ben Taylor developed during his.

After he retired, Taylor spent some time umpiring in the Negro Leagues; but broke his arm in a fall. It was not properly set and had to be amputated. However, he remained active in African American baseball. Taylor owned a company that printed and sold game programs and scorecards for the Baltimore Elite Giants during the 1940s. He died in Baltimore of pneumonia in 1953.

Ben Taylor's induction into the National Baseball Hall of Fame in 2006 honored his ability as a baseball player. But his presence was in Cooperstown before his induction. Buck Leonard's induction into the Hall of Fame in 1972 had been a testament to the coaching ability and character of his mentor; Ben Taylor.

CHAPTER 7

Cristobal Torriente

At 5'10" and a heavily muscled 190 pounds with broad shoulders, it was no wonder Negro League outfielder Cristobal Torriente was called "The Cuban Strongman". Torriente was known for consistently hitting a baseball over 400 feet. He coupled that with speed to catch line drives most outfielders could not get near and a strong arm to throw out base runners that challenged it. Not only seen along with fellow countrymen Martin Dihigo and Jose Mendez as the top Hispanic players in the Negro Leagues, many considered him one of black baseball's greatest outfielders.

Indianapolis ABCs' manager CI Taylor said of Torriente, "There walks a ball club!" The highest compliment of a baseball players' ability comes from his competition. The Chicago American Giants and Taylor's team had a fierce rivalry. Playing for the Giants, Torriente participated in many of the hotly contested games between the two teams and Taylor based his comment on what he saw firsthand. The ABCs' manager viewed the player's versatility and ability to carry a team on his broad Cuban shoulders. Torriente could play any outfield position, second base or third base, and he could pitch if necessary. Teams found it difficult to set up their defenses when he batted. The left handed slugger could hit the ball with power to all fields. Sufficient statistics are known to say with certainty Torriente had home run power and hit for a high average throughout his career.

Pitchers had a hard time getting him out due to his quick, powerful swing. They could not throw strikes pass him. Getting him to swing at pitches out of the strike zone also did not work because the Cuban was a notorious bad ball hitter. Facing him was an experience pitchers dreaded.

Many stories have been told as a testimony of the Cuban's power when batting. One is about a line drive he hit off the right field wall in Indianapolis against the ABCs. Supposedly the ball was hit so hard, it got to the wall so fast, the right fielder was able to throw the speedy Torriente out at first base. Another story is about a ball he supposedly hit in Kansas City against the Monarchs. It smashed a clock 17 feet above the centerfield fence. According to Torriente's American Giant teammate shortstop Bob Williams, "The hand of the clock started going round and round." It is doubtful all the stories of balls hit by Torriente are true. But there is no doubt he was one of the best hitters seen by Negro League fans.

Little is known about the early life of Cristobal Torriente in Cuba. From most information, he was born in 1893 in Cienfuegos. His family worked in the fields and boiler houses of the area's sugar mills. By 17 he was in the Cuban Army displaying his physical strength by loading heavy guns onto mules; while also blasting baseballs around local sandlots.

After being a young phenomenon in the 1913 Cuban Winter League, the 19 year old Torriente joined the Cuban Stars and played his first season in the United States. The Stars were a traveling team that played mainly against independent black professional baseball teams. No official African American league existed at the time, but the Stars competed against such black teams as the New York Lincoln Giants, New York Lincoln Stars, Chicago American Giants, and others. The change in surroundings did not hinder Torriente. He quickly began to establish himself as the team's hitting star going up against the likes of "Smokey Joe" Williams, "Cannonball" Dick Redding, "Big Bill" Gatewood, and other Negro League pitchers. By many accounts, Torriente hit .383 that first year. And if the Stars' opponents believed that was just rookie luck, the strong Cuban put that to rest the next season by again hitting over .300. In his years with the Cuban Stars, he reportedly never hit less than .300.

After the end of the 1913 season in the United States, Torriente returned home to play in the winter league. A reflection of the sport's popularity in the country, the league was a competitive blend of Cuban and other Latin Americans along with both Negro League and existing Major League players trying to make money in the off season. Due to resentment for the United States' interference in their country after the Spanish-American War, Cuban baseball fans loved to see their countrymen outplay Americans. Only in his early 20's, Torriente's journey down the road to becoming a baseball legend in his homeland had already begun. Stories of him hitting over .400 year after year in winter baseball followed him on returning to the United States.

In the summer of 1916 Torriente left the Cuban Stars to play for All Nations, a multi-racial barnstorming team founded by future Kansas City Monarch owner J. L. Wilkerson. All Nations travelled throughout the upper Midwest playing local white semi-professional and black professional teams. Negro League pitching star John Donaldson and Torriente's fellow countryman Jose Mendez were also on that year's team; said to be one of All Nation's best. They swept a three game series from the Indianapolis ABCs and won one out of three against the powerful Chicago American Giants that year. Torriente returned to the Cuban Stars the next season.

His explosive temper created a blemish to his great play on the field. It erupted during a game in 1917 when he got into a fight with Sam Crawford, manager of the Detroit Stars. Supposedly, they tussled on the field for 25 minutes and continued the confrontation after leaving the ballpark. Only hours later when the police arrested them both did it end. Torriente's temper would cause him more problems in the latter stages of his career.

At the end of World War I, Chicago was becoming an urban mecca for African Americans. The lure of the possibility for economic stability and a better life had fueled the migration of southern blacks to the city. Rube Foster used the growing aura Chicago had for African Americans to attract ballplayers to his Chicago American Giants. He felt the city gave him an advantage when talking to a player about joining his team. Other owners accused Foster of using what Chicago was becoming for African Americans to steal their ballplayers. Foster's approach proved successful with Torriente, who went to play for the American Giants in 1918. He had excellent seasons with the Cuban Stars, however it would be with Foster's team that Torriente would reach his peak as a baseball player.

Having the most area to cover, centerfield is the most challenging outfield position. Most managers choose their fastest outfielder to play it. This was Rube Foster's thinking in regards to Cristobal Torriente. Although the Cuban mostly played right field in his years with the Cuban Stars, his speed and strong arm were a perfect fit for centerfield in Foster's mind. With Torriente as the anchor in centerfield, the American Giants went on to have a consistently good outfield for many years. Good ballplayers such as Hall of Famer Oscar Charleston, Jimmy Lyons, Floyd "Jelly" Gardner, and David Malarcher all shared the American Giants' outfield at one time or another with Torriente.

When Rube Foster's vision became a reality in 1920 and the Negro National League (NNL) was formed, his Chicago American Giants became its premier team from the start. They won the league championship the first three years (1920 – 1922). The lack of documented league statistics prevents a true picture from being given of Torriente's performance on the field during the American Giants' years of dominance. Research indicates he finished those seasons hitting from .342 to as high as .411. Clearly, they were his best seasons in the Negro Leagues.

The events in his homeland after the 1920 season would contribute to Torriente's legacy as a ballplayer. The New York Giants came to Havana in October after the 1920 Major League season to play in a three team tournament. The team was led by Hall of Fame infielder Frankie Frisch and John McGraw was the manager. One of the other teams in the tournament, Almendares, would have Torriente playing in centerfield. The tournament promoter had also invited Babe Ruth to play with the Giants. Ruth had hit fifty-four home runs for the New York Yankees that season and would be a drawing card in Cuba. Supposedly, he was offered $2,000 per game to play with the Giants in the tournament.

November 5, 1920 is one of the most memorable days in Cuban baseball history. A part of Cuban baseball lore, it is said on that day Cristobal Torriente outhit the great Babe Ruth three home runs to none. Another account of the day's activities said the big Cuban hit one of the home runs off the Babe. So many versions have been told it is hard to separate the truth from myth. Torriente did hit three home runs that day, but not against Giant pitchers. Not bringing all of their pitchers to Cuba for the games, the Giants used players from other positions to pitch. On that day, Torriente hit three home runs off third baseman George "High Pockets" Kelly.

It is true Ruth pitched to Torriente in that game. Before coming to the Yankees, the Babe had pitched for the Boston Red Sox. In the one inning he pitched, Ruth gave up a double to Torriente whose team won 11 – 4.

After the 1925 season, the American Giants decided to split with their Cuban star. Torriente's temper and love of the Chicago night life caused disagreements with the strict team discipline set by Rube Foster. The centerfielder was not keeping in the best physical shape and his batting average had dropped to the .260s. Rumors were whispered that his skills were deteriorating, although he was only 31 years old. Rather than go through another difficult season with him, the American Giants traded Torriente to the Kansas City Monarchs.

The Monarchs appeared to be an ideal fit for him. The team's owner, J. L. Wilkerson, also owned the team Torriente had played on in 1916; All Nations. In addition, his fellow countryman and former All Nations' teammate Jose Mendez was the Monarchs' manager. The center fielder responded well on the field to the familiar faces in his new environment. He regained his hitting stroke and batted over .340. However, the team still had problems with him. A lover of fine jewelry, Torriente quit the team briefly after his expensive diamond ring was displaced. He eventually sued the Monarchs, accusing the team's trainer of losing it. After his anger about the ring subsided, Torriente returned to help the Monarchs battle the American Giants for the league pennant. His former team won the championship playoff five games to four behind the pitching of Hall of Famer Willie Foster, Rube's half-brother.

A portion of the credit for Torriente's comeback season went to the Monarchs' manager Jose Mendez, who was a positive influence for the centerfielder. But Mendez retired after the playoffs and returned to Cuba. His leaving may have played a part in the Monarchs' decision to release Torriente before the 1927 season.

Torriente spent the next two years with the Detroit Stars, batting over .300 in 1927. However, nagging injuries plagued him next season as his body began to breakdown. He was no longer "the Cuban strongman". After the 1928 season, he played the remainder of his career with lower level, semi-pro black teams.

After retiring from baseball in 1932, Torriente did not go back to Cuba. He resided in New York City, living in poverty and battling alcoholism. He died of tuberculosis on April 11, 1938 and was returned to his homeland for burial. In 1939 he was one of the first players inducted into the Cuban Baseball Hall of Fame.

During Cristobal Torriente's time in Negro League baseball, there were Cubans with his light skin complexion playing in the Major Leagues. They were able to blend in with the white players. But Torriente never crossed the "invisible color line". Major League scouts and managers certainly knew of his talents. Many Major League players saw with their own eyes in the Cuban winter league his baseball abilities. The problem, some believed, was the Cuban's hair. Torriente's teammate with the Chicago American Giants Jelly Gardner said, "The New York Giants scouted and liked him. They would have signed him, but his hair was too kinky." According to Gardner, Torriente was kept out of the Major Leagues because his hair could not hide that he was a black player. This assessment, true or false, showed the depth of the negative racial climate that was in baseball for nearly half of the 20th Century.

Before being elected to the National Baseball Hall of Fame in 2006, Cristobal Torriente had already received high consideration as a ballplayer. Torriente along with Martin Dihigo and Jose Mendez were the top Cubans to play in the Negro Leagues. In an early 1950s poll of former Negro League players and sportswriters, he was named one of the best outfielders to play Negro League baseball. But Torriente's 2006 induction into the Hall of Fame goes further than those considerations It gives him a place as one of the best outfielders to play the game period.

CHAPTER 8

Andy Cooper

"He was an exception to the rule", is an overused cliché. But in Andy Cooper's case, it was more than just a flippant, commonly used phrase. It was the truth and it landed him a plaque in the National Baseball Hall of Fame.

The most notable pitchers in the Negro Leagues were typified by the power and speed behind their pitches. Throwing the baseball so hard and fast, those pitchers overpowered the batter most of the time. Hitters could not swing the bat quick enough to make solid contact with the ball, if they hit it at all. In his prime, Hall of Famer Satchel Paige's fastball was described by batters as being the size of a half dollar or a pea. By the nickname given other pitchers, the batters knew what to expect when facing them. "Smokey" Joe Williams, "Cannonball" Dick Redding, Wilber "Bullet" Rogan, and "Steel Arm" Johnny Taylor were just a few whose name preceded their pitches. Using radar technology to gauge the speed of pitches was not introduced into baseball until the 1970s. However, if it had been used to clock the pitches of the great Negro League baseball hurlers, it would have registered at ninety-plus miles per hour many times.

But Andrew Lewis Cooper was a different kind of pitcher. He did not overpower batters. "Lefty", as he was nicknamed, used a variety of pitches at different speeds to get batters out.

In order to hit the ball solidly, a batter must have balanced coordination and timing between his legs, waist, shoulders, and hands. If a pitcher can disrupt that coordination and timing, getting the hitter swinging too early or too late; it usually leads to a fly out, groundout or strike out. Andy Cooper was a master of keeping hitters off balance. Not having the blazing fastball like other great Negro League pitchers, he had the ability to get batters out by disrupting their coordination and timing. "Lefty" had a successful career by frustrating and foiling them with his arsenal of pitches.

At 6'2", 220 pounds, Cooper had the build of a hard throwing, power pitcher. But batters soon learned not to look for smoking fast balls from "Lefty". Instead, he fed them an array of exceptional and effective breaking pitches: curveballs (curved or dropped from left to right), sliders (horizontal movement to right or left), screwballs (curved from right to left) and change ups (slower pitches from same pitching motion). Cooper could throw all his pitches at different speeds and had excellent control of them. When facing the lefthander, a batters' mind was confused as Cooper could mix up his pitches and locate them anywhere around home plate; especially the outside corner. The only left handed Negro League pitcher considered better than Andy Cooper was Hall of Famer Willie Foster.

Born 1896 in Waco, Texas, Cooper was a member of Negro League baseball's Texas fraternity; Willie Wells (Austin), Hilton Smith (Lincoln which is north of Giddings), Louis Santop (Tyler), Rube Foster (Winchester), and others. Information about his early life in Texas is scarce. However, prior to 1920, there were many semi-professional black baseball teams in Texas that helped to develop the future Negro League players from the state. Santop played with the Fort Worth Wonders, "Smokey" Joe Williams (Seguin, Texas) for the San Antonio Black Broncos, and Biz Mackey (Eagle Pass, Texas) for the San Antonio Black Aces are a few examples. In 1916, a short lived league was formed, the Colored Texas League, which included a team from Waco, Cooper's hometown.

Although little specific information is available, it is not illogical to infer Andy Cooper's baseball skills were honed on the sandlots around Waco and the black semi-professional baseball environment in Texas. However, it is certain that wherever Cooper was pitching as the 1920s began, he got the attention of the Detroit Stars.

The first official league for black baseball, the Negro National League (NNL) had its inaugural season in 1920. The Stars, owned by Detroit numbers operator Tenny Blount, were one of the league's charter teams. Hall of Fame outfielder Pete Hill also played for Detroit that first year. The Stars' home ballpark, Mack Park, had short outfield dimensions. It was said to be a hitter's paradise. A batter did not have to hit the ball far to get an extra base hit or home run. Cooper had difficulty making the needed adjustments to pitch effectively in such a park. The Stars' game statistics that have been discovered show him being less than a .500 pitcher the first two years.

That changed in 1922 as Cooper began to work his magic on the pitching mound. He became one of the best pitchers in the NNL that decade (1920s) rivaling Willie Foster and "Bullet" Rogan. Although classified as not official, some research has him winning at least 70 games between 1922 and 1928; but not all against NNL competition. Teams still tried to fit exhibition games into the league schedule to make extra money. This was a testament to the durability of Cooper and other Negro League pitchers. The NNL scheduled teams to play five game series starting Saturday through Tuesday, opposing teams would see Cooper in three of those five games. He would normally start two games and relieve in one. Even though he may have pitched many innings the previous day, "Lefty" could still pitch to a few batters in situations to preserve a win for the Stars.

Cooper also had a quick pick off move to first base that kept base runners close to the bag. Speed on the base paths, one important aspect of Negro League baseball, could cause havoc for pitchers. When a runner got on first base, there was a good chance he would steal second to get into scoring position. But base runners knew to beware of "Lefty". Planning to steal, if they got too far off first base, Cooper would pick them off.

The Kansas City Monarchs consistently finished at the top of the NNL the first half of the 1920s. They won the league pennant three straight years; 1923 – 1925. The team fell off the next two years, finishing second, and owner J. L. Wilkinson wanted to get them back on top. He had seen his team battle Andy Cooper year after year and knew the talented left hander could help the Monarchs to win another pennant. After the 1927 season, Wilkinson traded multiple Monarchs including popular slugger Hurley McNair to the Stars for Cooper. With the addition of "Lefty", the Monarchs were on top of the NNL again in 1929.

Injury cut the 1930 season short for Cooper. In a car accident with five teammates, he received severe cuts on his arms and legs. By the time he recovered near the season's end, he was not with the Monarchs. To help in the Stars attempt to win its first NNL pennant, the team had gotten Cooper back from Kansas City. However, Detroit lost the playoff series against the St. Louis Stars.

Just as Cooper returned to the Monarchs in 1931, the team pulled out of the NNL. With the death of Rube Foster and the national economic depression, the league faced financial instability.

To not be affiliated with any league is what Monarchs' owner J. L. Wilkinson believed the best way his team could survive the economic problems facing Negro League baseball. This would allow him to set the team's own schedule to play as many games as possible to generate revenue. The NNL shut down after the 1931 season.

No longer affiliated with any league, the Monarchs played all levels of competition travelling in the country's heartland from Canada to Mexico. Hall of Famers Turkey Stearnes and "Bullet" Rogan were a few of the notable players on the team along with Cooper in 1934. At 38 years old, he was still an effective pitcher and became the ace of the staff. Elected to pitch in the 1936 Negro League East-West All Star Game, Cooper gave up one hit in the one inning he pitched

As the Monarchs became a part of the new Negro American League (NAL) in 1937, Wilkinson named Cooper the team manager. Under Cooper, they won the league's first pennant. When needed, "Lefty" still pitched well enough to get batters out. This was quite an achievement considering he was 41 years old.

With Cooper at the helm the Monarchs also won NAL pennants in 1939 and 1940. He was a players' manager, handling the team with an easy going manner. Cooper trusted his players, expecting them to have a responsible and professional approach to their jobs. His players described him as being stern, but not too tough and not the type of manager that always criticized them.

Young players, especially pitchers, benefited from having Cooper as a teacher and father figure. He had a hand in the development of Hall of Fame pitcher Hilton Smith who began his professional career with the Monarchs. Smith said, "Andy Cooper was a smart manager, a great teacher – great teacher!" Also, Buck O'Neil learned the nuances of the game under Cooper, his first manager when coming to the Monarchs in 1938. O'Neil managed the Monarchs from 1948 - 1955 and credits what he learned from "Lefty" for preparing him for the job. "Andy Cooper was the best manager I have ever played for. He was an outstanding human being," said O'Neil.

An example of the high regard for Cooper was his selection to manage in the East-West All Star Game, the annual national showcase for Negro League baseball. In 1938 he led the West squad to a 5-4 victory; their first win in the summer classic in two years. Not so fortunate in 1940, Cooper's West squad lost 11 – 0.

While in Kansas City before spring training began in 1941, Andy Cooper had a stroke. In hopes of his recovery, the Monarchs named Newt Allen as interim manager. Cooper went back to Waco and never came back. "Lefty" died of heart failure in June. He did not live to see his Monarchs win the NNL Championship for a third straight year.

Elated to hear of his father's election into the National Baseball Hall of Fame in 2006, Andy Cooper, Jr. received tons of questions from news media people wanting to know more information about "Lefty". Many of those inquiries he could not answer being only 11 years old when his father died. However, he got help through a phone call from Negro League baseball's greatest ambassador; Buck O'Neil. Andy Cooper, Jr. became much more knowledgeable about his father after talking to O'Neil.

There were others who could have made that phone call. To his teammates on the Detroit Stars, to his opponents, and to his teammates and players he managed on the Kansas City Monarchs, there was nothing enigmatic about Andy Cooper. They knew him as a good teammate, a crafty left handed pitcher, and a successful baseball manager. Cooper did not have the aura of Satchel Paige or the notable reputation as some of the other good Negro League pitchers. There are no stories of Cooper that are a part of Negro League lore. However, enough opinions, documented statistics, and relevant information were available to get a true measure of Andy Cooper's baseball talent and garnished him a plaque in Cooperstown.

CHAPTER 9

Raleigh Mackey

In his Negro League baseball career Biz Mackey wore many hats. There is not much he did not do. Mackey is recognized as one of the best catchers in Negro League baseball history. An All-Star, a batting champion, a player on championship winning teams, a championship winning manager, and a mentor of Hall of Fame players, all describe Mackey's achievements. There are not many legendary stories about the feats of Biz Mackey that have been passed down through the years. However, his 2006 induction into the National Baseball Hall of Fame indicates the depth and mastery of his baseball abilities.

Webster's Dictionary defines a catcher as "the baseball player whose position is behind home plate and who signals for and receives pitches." But Biz Mackey went beyond Webster's definition. At 6'0" and 200 pounds, he had a catcher's body. However, Mackey moved around home plate with the quickness and agility of a smaller man.

He had no equal when it came to his defensive ability. Whether blocking pitches in the dirt, shifting his feet to catch pitches wide of the plate, or blocking home plate while tagging out base runners, Biz Mackey did it with style and grace. There were better hitting catchers in the Negro Leagues, but none better at playing the position.

Base stealers had to beware of Mackey's main calling card, his throwing arm. Powerful and deadly accurate, few catchers had a better one. Many said Biz could throw the ball to second base while in his catcher's crouch harder, quicker, and with more accuracy than most catchers could while standing up. He threw the ball with a short, quick motion without drawing his arm far back. Catchers called it the "snap throw". Mackey had it mastered enabling him to throw out the league's best base stealers.

Being behind home plate with all the action on the field in front of him, Biz developed a "sixth" sense for the game. He studied the hitters and knew their strengths and weaknesses. Knowing the mental makeup of his pitchers, he could get the best out of them. His battery mates during his career include such good pitchers as Webster McDonald, Jesse "Nip" Winters, and Hall of Famer Leon Day. For each batter Mackey would change the defensive alignment of his teammates in the field according to his pitcher's strengths and the hitter's weakness. This prepared him to be a manager in the latter stage of his career.

Although best known for his catching, Mackey deserves more credit as a hitter than he has received. Teammate Judy Johnson said about Biz's hitting, "He would sting the ball, but pitchers did not fear him. They would not walk him to get to somebody else." Mackey did not hit 400 feet home runs like Louis Santop or Josh Gibson, who were also catchers. However some information indicates the switch hitting catcher hit over .300 the first half of his career; capturing the Eastern Colored League (ECL) batting championship in 1923. The Hilldale Club of Darby, Pennsylvania defeated the Kansas City in the 1925 Negro League World Series with Biz Mackey as the team's hitting star.

The stereotypical chattering catcher, Biz would try to disrupt hitters by engaging in friendly conversation. He knew the tactics were working if he got a smile from the batter.

Eagle Pass, Texas is a small town south of Del Rio near the Mexican border. Here on July 27, 1897 James Raleigh "Biz" Mackey opened his eyes the first time. This makes him another member of the Texas fraternity of Negro League ballplayers from the Lone Star state; that includes Andy Cooper, Willie Wells, Rube Foster, Louis Santop, and others. Before becoming a teenager he moved with his family to Luling which is east of San Antonio on the road to Houston. The Mackeys were sharecroppers. Biz, along with his brothers, worked on the farm most of the day and then played baseball until dark. They used boards as bats and anything they could find as a ball. By 1916 the black amateur baseball team in Luling, the Oilers, had three Mackey brothers on its roster; Ray, Ernest, and Biz.

The San Antonio Aces, a black minor league team, signed Biz in 1918. Charlie Bellinger, the Aces' owner, had a friendship with Indianapolis ABCs' manager CI Taylor. Bellinger always looked for good ballplayers in Texas that would help Taylor's team. After the Aces folded in 1919, he sold Mackey and five other players to the ABCs.

Biz arrived in Indianapolis at the perfect time. The first official African American baseball league, the Negro National League (NNL), formed in 1920 with the ABCs one of the charter teams. The twenty-three year old Texan shared the dugout his first year with Hall of Famers Oscar Charleston and Ben Taylor, along with

"Cannonball" Dick Reading. Used as a utility infielder and outfielder, Mackey also began to learn the craft of playing the game under the master teacher, CI Taylor. With his manager's help, Biz became a switch hitter and developed into one of the team's top run producers. Some records show he hit over .300 each of his three years in Indianapolis, helping the team finish second in 1921.

CI Taylor died before that year ended, replaced by his brother Ben as the ABCs' manager. However, with his mentor CI gone, Mackey's ties to the team were loosened. The owners of the newly formed Eastern Colored League (ECL) in 1923 looked to lure away NNL players. Accepting an offer from Ed Bolden, owner of the Hilldale Club, Biz headed east without hesitation.

Already one of the top black teams on the east coast, Bolden's team was stronger going into the new league with the addition of Mackey. Biz split playing time with two aging Hall of Famers at two different positions his first year with the team: at shortstop with John Henry "Pop" Lloyd and as catcher with Louis Santop. A surprisingly good defense shortstop despite lacking speed, Biz could handle ground balls within his reach.

Hilldale won the first three ECL pennants. In 1924, they played the Kansas City Monarchs of the NNL for the first Negro League World Series Championship. Lloyd had left the team after the previous season, leaving Biz as the starting shortstop. However, an error in the series by Louis Santop changed the direction of Mackey's career. With the best five of nine games tied at three apiece and Hilldale one out away from winning a fourth game, Santop dropped a fly foul ball. Given new life with that error, the Monarchs rallied to win the game and went on the win the Series.

The next season Hilldale management decided Santop, at one time considered the best catcher in the Negro Leagues, had passed his prime and the team would be better off with Biz behind the plate. They did not regret that decision. Mackey hit over .340 and Hilldale captured the 1925 ECL pennant. They were pitted once again against the Kansas City Monarchs in the Negro League World Series, but the outcome would be different than the previous year due in part to Biz. He knocked in the leading run in the first game, scored the winning run in another, and got three hits the final game as Hilldale became the 1925 Series Championship. Mackey hit .360 for the series overall.

Biz played baseball year round. In the California Winter League, the first American professional league since the turn of the century to allow black and white players to compete against each other, he went up against Tony Lazzeri, Babe Herman, and other Major Leaguers. The teams were not integrated, but all black teams were allowed to participate. Along with a group of other black players, Mackey made at least three barnstorming trips to Japan during the 1920s and 1930s. Well received by Japanese baseball fans, the trips helped to develop professional leagues in the country. Biz played in Japan for the entire 1932 season.

Upon returning to the United States in 1933, Mackey needed a new team. His former team, Hilldale, had dissolved. However, its owner Ed Bolden put together a new team, the Philadelphia Stars. He recruited many of his former Hilldale players. At 36, Mackey could not hit as he did when younger, but still had his magic behind the plate. Along with Biz, Bolden got Hall of Famer Jud "Boojum" Wilson, Dick Lundy, Webster McDonald, and others to play for the Stars.

His playing in Japan the entire 1932 season did not decrease Mackey's popularity with Negro League fans. He received more votes from them than any other catcher for the first Negro League East-West All-Star in 1933, including Josh Gibson. In the national showcase game for black baseball, Biz got one hit in three at bats. Fans picked him for five All-Star games during his career, mainly for his defensive ability.

With the original NNL and the ECL gone, the Philadelphia Stars were part of a new league in 1934; the Negro National Association of Baseball Clubs. It would also be known as the NNL. The team won the new league's first championship and Biz Mackey's second. He batted .368 in the playoff series against the Chicago American Giants and drove in the first run in the deciding Seventh Game.

Still considered one of the league's best catchers even at 40 years old, Mackey began the 1937 season with the Washington

Generals. The team moved to Baltimore the next season and became the Elite Giants. Mackey then began the player/manager phase of his time in the Negro Leagues.

His first year in Baltimore, Mackey took under his wing a teenaged catcher from Philadelphia, Roy Campanella. Discovering the kid playing with a semi-professional Philadelphia black team the previous year, Biz persuaded Campanella's parents to allow their teenaged son to play with his team in Baltimore on weekends by promising to return him in time for school on Mondays. Mackey passed along all he knew about catching to the eager youngster. When Campanella had a Hall of Fame career in the Major Leagues, he gave credit to his former manager. Negro League fans said when you saw Campy operate behind the plate, you saw Biz Mackey.

In a one game playoff, the Elite Giants defeated the Homestead Grays to win the 1939 NNL pennant; the third championship for Mackey. But he left Baltimore to join the Newark Eagles in 1940. Newark team owners Abe and Effa Manley named him manager in 1941. With Monte Irvin, Leon Day, Lennie Pearson, Max Manning, and Biz still handling the catching at age 44, the Eagles had the makings of a good team. But, Mrs. Manley did not like Mackey's "small ball" approach to the game (bunt, hit and run, base stealing) and fired him after the season.

There is no record of Biz playing or coaching baseball anywhere for the next three years. But he resolved the conflict with Effa Manley and she renamed him as the Eagles' manager in 1945. With Monte Irvin returning from the Army and a young Larry Doby playing second base, the Eagles won the 1946 NNL pennant and defeated the Kansas City Monarchs to win the Negro League World Series; Biz Mackey's fourth championship.

When Negro League baseball began declining after Jackie Robinson and other African American players integrated the Major Leagues, the Manley's sold their team and it relocated to Houston, Texas in 1950. After one season with the team in Houston, near Luling where he first began playing organized baseball, Biz Mackey retired from the game and worked as a forklift operator in Los Angeles.

After playing over 30 years in the Negro Leagues, Biz Mackey's baseball career received deserving appreciation and he got the opportunity to experience a portion of it. In a poll by the Pittsburgh Courier in the early 1950s, Negro League fans and black newspaper sportswriters voted Biz ahead of Josh Gibson as the Negro Leagues' greatest catcher. In 1959 when the Los Angeles Dodgers honored Roy Campanella, who had been paralyzed from a car accident the previous year, Biz received acknowledgment and recognition as Campy's catching mentor. The Los Angeles Memorial Coliseum crowd of 93,000 gave Mackey a roaring ovation.

Biz Mackey did not live to see the crowning recognition of his baseball career, his 2006 induction into the National Baseball Hall of Fame. He died on September 27, 1965. Racial prejudice excluded him from being on the same playing field with Gabby Harnett, Bill Dickey, and Mickey Cochrane all considered the best catchers in the Major Leagues during the span of Biz's Negro League career. But Mackey's 2006 Hall of Fame induction puts him in the same building with them and says he must be included as one of their era's great catchers.

CHAPTER 10

Jud Wilson

Jud Wilson could hit a baseball. It was a fact most white baseball fans did not know, but no secret to anyone who knew about Negro League baseball. Jud Wilson could hit and he had the nickname to prove it.

The most telling assessment of a baseball player's ability comes from his fellow ballplayers. A player's opponents and his teammates know his talents and abilities. The great Hall of Fame pitcher Satchel Paige called Jud Wilson one of the best hitters he ever faced. Also, Hall of Fame catcher and Wilson's Homestead Grays teammate Josh Gibson called him one of the best hitters in the game.

Negro League players called Jud Wilson, "Boojum"; the sound they heard when balls hit by Wilson whacked the outfield fence. The name stuck his entire career, Jud "Boojum" Wilson.

"They looked the same to me." That's what Wilson said about all pitchers he faced. Although Negro League game statistics were not diligently recorded or were lost, it has been determined Wilson's lifetime league batting average higher than .340.

In the national showcase for Negro League baseball, the East – West All Star Game, "Boojum" hit .455. He was selected by Negro League fans to play in the first three All Star Games, 1933 – 1935, in which he got five hits. In the inaugural game, Wilson got two of the East All Stars' seven hits off Willie Foster and drove in three of their seven runs. The West All Stars won the game 11 – 7. Wilson drove in the winning run in the 1934 game with an 8th inning single.

But records show "Boojum" Wilson could hit more than Negro League pitching. He also batted .356 in 26 barnstorming exhibition games against white Major League pitchers and in Cuba during winter league games he hit over .400. He showed just as he said, "They all look the same to me".

At 5'8", 195 lbs., Wilson had a build like a wrestler. He had Herculean strength in his upper body with broad shoulder, muscular arms, and a tapered waist. Bowlegged and pigeon-toed, Wilson crowded home plate with his left handed batting stance and dared pitchers to hit him. With his bat cocked to hit, he posed an intimidating figure at home plate for whoever was on the mound.

Wilson hit line drives to every corner of the field. Whereas some hitters would be classified as better able to handle fastballs or curves, "Boojum" had no preference. He could hit them all. He was contact hitter with a high batting average and a power stroke.

As a fielder, Wilson did not have the skills of famous Negro League third basemen Judy Johnson and Ray Dandridge. Although not very graceful, he had good fielding instincts. Quick enough to knock down the ball to keep it in front of him and then throw out the runner, he had the reputation of being more than adequate playing both third and sometimes first base. Former teammate Jimmie Crutchfield said; "He was not a good third baseman, but he could play enough third base not to hurt you and he could hit everything in sight".

Wilson was a clutch, productive hitter for eight league championship teams and two Negro League World Series champions; another measure of his tremendous talent as a baseball player. He also played for two of the teams that get consideration as the greatest in Negro League history. Although not as heralded as Satchel Paige, Josh Gibson, Buck Leonard, and other Negro League great players, Jud "Boojum" Wilson could hit.

Born on February 28, 1899 in Remington, Virginia, Ernest Judson Wilson left the rural life of the "Old Dominion State" for Washington, DC. His baseball skills were cultivated on the sandlots of Washington's Foggy Bottom, an area flooded by African Americans migrating into the city during the early 1900s. After leaving military service in 1918, Wilson returned to play with black amateur teams around the nation's capital. In 1922 he began what would be a twenty-four year Negro League career by playing first for the Baltimore Black Sox. The next year the Black Sox were one of the charter teams in the new Eastern Colored League (ECL). Playing first and third base, Wilson was a consistent year to year .300 plus hitter for the team.

The infield of the 1929 Baltimore Black Sox: Jud Wilson first base, Frank Warfield second base, Oliver "Ghost" Marcelle third base, and "Sir" Dick Lundy shortstop, were proclaimed the "Million Dollar Infield" by the sports editors of black newspapers. A million dollars is what Wilson and the others would have been worth if they were white and all playing together on a Major League team. The Black Sox that year were champions of the American Negro League. This new league was formed with teams from the ECL that shutdown the previous year (Hilldale, Lincoln Giants, Cuban Stars, Bacharach Giants) and the Homestead Grays. It lasted only that one season.

When the economic condition of the Black Sox crumbled after the 1930 season, Wilson signed with the Homestead Grays. Along with him, that 1931 Grays team also had Josh Gibson, Ted Page, Oscar Charleston ,"Smokey" Joe Williams and Willie Foster. Wilson played third base and presided as team captain. Years later, Gibson said of all the teams he had played on, the 1931 Grays were the best. Many Negro League historians agree with Gibson as they see the team as one of black baseball's best.

The next year Gus Greenlee, the owner of the Pittsburgh Crawfords, lured Wilson, Gibson, and Charleston, away from the Grays by offering them more money. Their teammates on the 1932 Crawfords were Judy Johnson, "Cool Papa" Bell, and Satchel Paige. The team finished with a record of 99 wins and only 36 losses. With those six Hall of Famers on the roster, that Crawford team gets many votes as the best black team ever.

After one season with the Crawfords, Wilson signed with the Philadelphia Stars. Along with him on the Stars were former Black Sox teammate Dick Lundy and Hall of Fame catcher Raleigh "Biz" Mackey who had returned from playing baseball in Japan. The Stars were in the Negro National League (NNL) that had been resurrected by Pittsburgh Crawfords' owner Gus Greenlee in 1933. In 1934, Philadelphia faced the Chicago American Giants in a seven game championship playoff series. Chicago had Hall of Famers Willie Foster, Willie Wells, Norman "Turkey" Stearnes, and "Mules" Suttles, but Wilson and the Stars won the series to become NNL champions.

"Boojum" not only had a reputation for his potent bat, but also for his powerful fists. Described by friends as a genial person off the field, once "Boojum" put on his uniform he became a fiery-eyed, quick-tempered strong man. When he became angry, Wilson put fear in opponents, umpires, and even teammates. A fierce competitor, no one escaped his wrath when he got upset. He hated losing and willingly fought anyone and everyone when he believed it necessary.

Wilson constantly clashed with umpires. The lack of respect for umpires by the players surfaced as a major problem in the Negro Leagues many times. So bad at times umpires carried weapons for protection against possible harm from players. "Boojum" was an umpire's nightmare. He struck one during the 1934 Negro Championship Series while playing with the Philadelphia Stars. However, after hearing Wilson's threats of bodily harm if he tried to eject him, the umpire let him continue playing. Chicago American Giants' manager David Malarcher protested, but the umpire thought it better to hear his complaints than face the fury of Wilson's anger.

In a game against the Newark Eagles while playing with the Grays, "Boojum" took a third strike with the bases loaded as the final out in his team's lost. Upset because he thought the pitch should have been called ball four, Wilson found the umpire in the locker room and swung a bat at him. The umpire ducked at the last second. The other players restrained Wilson as the police got the umpire out of the room.

And there is the legendary story about Wilson's temper involving his friend Jake Stephens, a Philadelphia Star teammate in 1934. He and Stephens were roommates for an All Star in Chicago. After the game, Stephens came into the room making noise at 2:00 AM. The noise awoke the sleeping "Boojum" who became so upset he hung the smaller Stephens out the window of their sixteenth floor hotel room. In spite of his loud screams and frantic kicking, Stephens hung out the window until Wilson calmed down. The incident, though scary, did not destroy their friendship.

Wilson's personality allowed him still to get along with other players most of the time. Monte Irvin said, "You could kid with Boojum". But Irvin and everyone knew that during a closely fought game or a questionable call by an umpire, watch out! "Boojum" could explode.

Even in the latter stage of his career "Boojum" could still swing the bat. In the 1930s and 1940s, Negro League teams would play two and sometimes three games on weekend days and then travel by bus or car to the city of their next scheduled game. It meant many long, overnight drives, which at times became hazardous. In

1937, the Philadelphia Stars' bus collided with a car, seriously injuring Wilson who was the team's manager. This caused him to stop playing full time for two years. But Cum Posey, owner of the Homestead Grays, believed that even at 41 years old and not fully recovered from the injury, Jud Wilson could still hit. Upon joining the team in 1940, Wilson proved Posey right. 1940 – 1945 were great years for the Homestead Grays. The team won six Negro National League pennants and two Negro League World Series championships. The core players for the Grays included Josh Gibson, Buck Leonard, "Cool Papa" Bell, Raymond Brown, Roy Partlow and Jud "Boojum" Wilson. "Boojum" could still hit.

The last years of his career Wilson suffered from strange convulsions. During one game he fell to the ground around 3rd base and drew circles with his fingers in the dirt. Doctors finally diagnosed him with epilepsy. Hospitalized at times, Wilson could no longer be an everyday player. However, whenever he did play, he could still hit the baseball.

The racial barriers that kept African Americans out of Major League baseball crumbled too late for Jud Wilson. By the time Jackie Robinson began playing with the Brooklyn Dodgers in 1947, Wilson then at age 48 had retired. He remained in Washington D.C. until he died in 1963. Bedridden during his last days, he had trouble responding to his surroundings. However; when former teammate Judy Johnson mentioned the name Jake Stephens, Wilson remembered Stephens as his former roommate. There are even some accounts that Stephens actually visited Wilson during that time and they chatted as old friends.

Jud "Boojum" Wilson played his entire career in the Negro Leagues and many black sportswriters saw players like him as one of black baseball's problems. They believed his temper outbursts and physical assaults of umpires tarnished Negro League baseball's image. Some speculated black players like Wilson did not have the temperament to play in the Major Leagues. However, there were many white professional ballplayers with anger issues during the 1930s (Pepper Martin, Leo Durocher, etc.). Major League ballplayers were not all "choir boys". Many had alcohol addictions and other character issues that were just not publicized. Despite his quick temper, "Boojum" Wilson at least deserved a chance to make it in the Major Leagues, a chance to at least fail. But he did not get one.

Although Wilson received the Hall of Fame recognition he deserved in 2006, Major League fans never got to hear the "boojum" sound of a Jud Wilson line drive whacking the outfield wall. If they would have heard it, Wilson's nickname would have stuck even in Major Leagues. "Boojum!" "Boojum!"

CHAPTER 11

George Suttles

Teammates would say when Negro League power hitter George "Mule" Suttles swung his bat at a pitch they could feel the earth shake. "Kick Mule, Kick!", is what fans and teammates would chant when "Mule" came up to bat. The fifty ounce bat he swung was a testament to his strength. A low ball hitter, Suttles swung at every pitch with all his might to hit the ball out of the ballpark,; as his fans wanted him to do. Like most power hitters that over swung, he had a high number of strike outs each year. But more than frequently "Mule" connected hitting the ball a long way.

Because of the lack of documented Negro League baseball statistics, the total number of home runs hit by Suttles is not known. Supposedly, he led the Negro National League in round trippers twice. There is an eyewitness account of a 500 foot home run he hit over the centerfield fence at Griffith Stadium in Washington, D.C. Hall of Fame Negro Leaguer Willie Wells frequently told the story of a 600 foot home run "Mule" hit at Havana's Tropical Park while playing in the Cuban Winter League. The ball carried out of the stadium and over the heads of the Cuban soldiers on horseback doing crowd control duty behind the fence. Afterwards, a marker was supposedly placed at the spot the ball landed commemorating "Mule's" blast. Another version of that home run has it landing in the ocean.

Chico Renfro, former Kansas City Monarchs' infielder and longtime sports editor recalled, "Suttles had the rawest power of any player I've ever seen." Since the major white newspapers mainly ignored Negro League baseball, "Mule" was not included when the Major League power hitters of that time - Babe Ruth, Lou Gehrig, Hack Wilson, Jimmie Foxx, and others, were given national media recognition. However, "Mule" was popular among Negro League baseball fans because they knew the stories about his home run power.

There is conflicting information as to the origin of George Suttles' nickname "Mule". It comes from when he was a youth, a dispute about his birthplace. Some information says Suttles was born in Brockton, Louisiana on March 31, 1900 or 1901. It says the nickname came from his raising of mules while growing up on a farm. Other information says he was born in Blocton, Alabama and the nickname was due to the strength he developed working in the coal mines as a teenager. In either case, "strong as a mule" was the opinion others had of him throughout his 21 or 22 year Negro League career. Suttles accepted the name given him and in speaking of himself would say, "Don't worry about the Mule going blind, just load the wagon and give me the lines." Carrying the offensive load for his team is what "Mule" did many times. Like most big men he was slow on his feet in the field and not noted for his defensive skills as a first baseman and outfielder. But his offensive power helped win two league championships for the St. Louis Stars (1930, 1931).

The accounts of his actual size vary from being 6'3" to 6'6" and weighing 215 - 250 lbs. Suttles lost his temper and hit an umpire during the 1933 League Championship Series, but the action was out of character. Everyone knew "Mule" as a fun loving, gentle giant.

Whether born in Louisiana or Alabama, Suttles' first exposure to black baseball was in Birmingham. To escape the hard labor and limitations imposed by racial segregation, Birmingham's African American society turned to baseball as an outlet. While working in the coal mines near Alabama's capital city, Suttles and his brother Charles played baseball in a league of black teams sponsored by mining and other industrial companies. In 1920 the Birmingham Black Barons were formed from the best players in those industrial leagues. The Black Barons were first a minor league team playing in the Negro Southern League and was a point of pride for Birmingham's black community.

There is some indication the first Negro League uniform worn by "Mule" was a New York Bacharach Giants in 1922 when he was 21 years old. The circumstances surrounding his going to the Giants have not been detailed, but he did not see much time on the field and returned to Alabama.

In 1923 Charles Suttles broke his leg while working in a coal mine and missed his opportunity to play for the Black Barons. But the team signed "Mule" the same year and it became a part of the Negro National League (NNL) in 1924.

Starting as an outfielder, Suttles also began playing first base at times in 1925. His fielding at both positions was just barely adequate, but it was with his hitting that the big right handed swinger began to show potential. The few statistics recovered for his time with the Black Barons indicate he was one of the team's leading hitters for batting average and home runs.

Due to financial problems that plagued most Negro League baseball teams at that time, the Black Barons dropped out of the Negro National League after the 1925 season. This forced Suttles to make a move that changed his life. Hoping to escape racial segregation and looking for better economic opportunities many African Americans from southern states like Alabama moved to northern cities in the 1920's. "Mule" became a part of that vast migration in 1926. Although he had lived in the south all his life, Suttles left Birmingham to play for the St. Louis Stars. An original member of the NNL in 1920, the team was initially called the St. Louis Giants until the name was changed by its new owner in 1921.

The creation of "Mule" Suttles' legend as a home run slugger began as he played with the St. Louis Stars. Although there are many unsubstantiated tales of his long ball power while with the team, it is certainly true he was one of the Negro National League's top home run hitters from 1926 – 1931. One story tells of Suttles hitting three home runs in a game and the opposing team walking off the field when he came to bat the fourth time.

At Stars Park, the St. Louis Stars' home field, the distance from home plate to the left field fence was 269 feet. On the other side of the fence was a barn for trolley cars. It made the field hitter friendly for right handed batters like Suttles. But this does not tarnish "Mule's" home run totals. His raw physical strength and power enabled him to hit home runs to all fields; center, right, and left. No ballpark could hold the baseball when Suttles made a 400 and 500 feet connection with his bat.

Also, he was among the league leaders in doubles and triples while with the Stars. Many fans believe the triple is the most exciting hit in baseball. To see a big man like "Mule" Suttles running from home to third base with surprising speed was a treat for Negro League fans.

Along with Suttles, Hall of Famers Willie Wells and James "Cool Papa" Bell were a part of some very good St. Louis Stars teams. From 1926 – 1929 the Stars finished near the top of league standings before finally winning the pennant in both 1930 and 1931.

The Negro National League closed its doors after the 1931 season. With the country in the gripes of the worst economic depression in its history, Negro League fans could no longer afford tickets to see their favorite teams. Attendance at NNL games dropped to the level where teams did not have the money needed to keep operating. Despite their pennant winning season, the St. Louis Stars went out of business.

However, even in the face of the depression, Negro League baseball was determined to survive. Seeing themselves as professionals, Negro League ballplayers left home and family in pursuit of places to apply their professional skills.

A new league was formed in 1932; the East-West League (EWL). The teams in the EWL were the Newark Browns, Detroit Wolves, Homestead Grays, Baltimore Black Sox, Philadelphia Hilldale Giants, Washington Pilots, and Cleveland Bears. "Mule" Suttles, along with his former teammates with the St. Louis Stars Willie Wells and "Cool Papa" Bell, played for the Detroit team. By June, the team was battling for first place, but not enough fans were attending games and it shut down operations. Another EWL team, the Washington Pilots, picked up Suttles. However, shortly after "Mule" joined the team, the league shut down and the 1932 season was over. Negro League baseball and the career of "Mule" Suttles had reached a low point. But the circumstances for both would begin turning the next year.

Due to the efforts of Pittsburgh Crawford's owner Gus Greenlee, a new league was formed in 1933. The Negro National Association of Baseball Clubs was patterned after the first African American baseball league started by the late Rube Foster in 1920, retaining the former league's name of the Negro National League (NNL).

Greenlee financed his baseball team with money from illegal gambling activities; he operated the main "numbers racket" in Pittsburgh's black community. This was before the current existing state lotteries. Men like Greenlee operated an illegal numbers lottery that people paid money into daily, despite the tough financial times, for a chance to have the lucky winning number. Any set of numbers such as that day's stock market average, or other publicly announced numbers were predetermined as the winners.

It was a lucrative business for the "numbers" operators and many people saw men like Greenlee as mobsters that preyed on poor people by taking their hard earned cash for a small chance of them winning. However, there were others who saw nothing wrong in giving people the opportunity to win money they needed.

During the depression "numbers" operators like Greenlee were one of only a few businesses making money in African American communities. Since many of them were sportsmen also, like Greenlee they became a source of financing for many Negro League teams. In addition to Greenlee's Pittsburgh Crawfords, the Newark Eagles, Homestead Grays, New York Cubans, New York Black Yankees, and Nashville/Baltimore Elite Giants were owned or heavily financed by "numbers" operators in the 1930's.

The Chicago American Giants, Rube Foster's former team, was a member of the new NNL. Funeral home operator Robert Coles was the team's new owner. Not known as a strong baseball man, Coles was smart enough to add "Mule" Suttles to the team for the 1933 season. Both Negro League baseball and "Mule" were operating once again and both of their circumstances were going to get even better that season.

The NNL held its first East-West All-Star Game on September 10, 1933. It was the brainchild of Greenlee and two black newspaper sportswriters, Roy Sparrow of the Pittsburgh Sun-Telegraph and Bill Nunn of the Pittsburgh Courier. It was played in Chicago's Comiskey Park where Major League baseball had its first All Star Game earlier that summer.

The event was designed to be a national showcase for Negro League baseball. Fans could use ballots in the Pittsburgh Courier, Chicago Defender, and other black newspapers to vote for their favorite player. "Mule" Suttles received 35,134 votes from fans for the inaugural East-West All Star Game. It was a tremendous success as fans came from around the country dressed in their Sunday best to see the game. With 19,568 attending the game, it was one of the largest gatherings of African Americans for that time. "Mule" lived up to his nickname by hitting a double and the first East-West All-

Star Game home run in the West All-Stars' 11 – 7 victory. Compared to the previous year, 1933 was tremendous for both "Mule" and black baseball.

The East-West All-Star Game became an annual affair and Negro League baseball's most successful event. It was where top black society yearly got together, where the top clothing fashions were seen. The players saw it as more than an exhibition game. It was an honor to be elected to participate and the players approached the game with a competitive attitude. Satchel Paige, Josh Gibson, Oscar Charleston, Buck Leonard, and other Negro League greats played in the yearly classic. So did future Major League stars Jackie Robinson, Larry Doby, Roy Campanella, and others.

It was the biggest stage for Negro League ballplayers to perform, and few performed on it better than "Mule". In addition to his great hitting in the first All-Star Game in 1933, he got three hits in the 1934 game. But, it was the 1935 game that "Mule's" star really shined. While playing in the outfield, Suttles moved his big body fast enough to make a shoestring catch in the top of the 11th inning. That defensive gem kept the score tied at 8 – 8. With two on in the bottom of the same inning, he hit a home run off of Martin Dihigo to win the game for the West All-Stars 11 – 8. In five All-Star Games, "Mule" Suttles batted .412 with two home runs and six runs batted in.

Despite his success in the 1935 East West All-Star Game, "Mule" Suttles was beginning to show signs of age. At 34 years old, he did not have the quick bat swing as when he was younger and pitchers were able to get him out more frequently with their fast ball. Also, he was becoming increasingly less mobile which had a negative effect on his defensive skills. To add to the physical changes at that point in his career, "Mule" would have to be on the move to continue playing. Due to financial problems, the American Giants had trouble paying their players and dropped out of the NNL after the 1935 season.

Still believing he had more baseball in him, 'Mule" signed on with the Newark Eagles in 1936. Owned by Abe Manley, a businessman and reported "numbers operator", the team was operated by his wife, Effa. It was formed that year when the Manley's merged their previous team, the Brooklyn Eagles, with a team they purchased, the Newark Dodgers.

Although Suttles' defensive skills at first base were wanting, he became a part of what black sportswriters called the Eagles' "Million Dollar Infield": Dick Seay played second base, Suttles' former teammate Willie Wells was at shortstop, and Ray Dandridge played third. On any Major League team the sportswriters believed the combined talent of those players was worth a million dollars. Hall of Famer Leon Day, Max Manning, and a young Monte Irvin were also on that team.

Despite his advancing age while with the Eagles, Suttles still was a dangerous hitter for pitchers to face. Although no longer hitting for a high batting average, "Mule" still had enough power to hit the ball out of the park. If a pitcher was not careful and threw a pitch that Suttles could quickly get his bat around, the "Mule" could still kick it. He helped the Eagles battle the Homestead Grays and Baltimore Elite Giants for NNL supremacy from 1936 – 1941. Elected to play in the East-West All-Star Game in 1937 – 1939, he was still popular with Negro League fans.

Due to injuries from which "Mule" and Ray Dandridge were both trying to recover, the Manley's decided to not let the players participate in the 1938 game. Josh Gibson was also hurt and held for the game. The East All-Star team lost 5 – 4 and their fans blamed it on the absence of Dandridge, Gibson, and "Mule".

The Manley's traded Suttles to the New York Black Yankees in 1941, but brought him back the next season. In 1943 the Manley's gave "Mule" the reins to manage the team. However, the nucleus of the strong Eagles' teams of the late 1930's was gone. Both Ray Dandridge and Willie Wells had left to play in the Mexican League for more money. Monte Irvin was serving in the military. Under Suttles the team did not have the prominent status it had before World War II.

After the 1944 season "Mule" retired. Other than being one of the twenty former players that became Negro League umpires after retirement, he unnoticeably lived the remainder of his life in Newark. Suffering from cancer, Suttles died in 1968.

Former teammate on the Eagles' Lennie Pearson says that "Mule" would tell the young players, "When I die have little thought for my memory, but do not mourn me too much." The memories George "Mule" Suttles left for baseball fans to ponder takes more than a "little thought." Despite large amounts of Negro League game statistics being absent, enough is known to conclude that "Mule" Suttles was one of the most feared sluggers in Negro League baseball history. Josh Gibson has been declared the Negro Leagues all-time home run king. "Mule" may not have hit as many home runs as Gibson, but he hit the ball as far.

There is enough information known to indicate Suttles hit well against Major Leaguer pitchers in barnstorming exhibitions, Cuban winter league games, and in the California Winter League contests. Could he have been like Jimmie Foxx, Hack Wilson, or Chuck Klein, his slugging contemporaries at the time who were in the Major Leagues? This question can only be pondered due to the racial discrimination that did not give Suttles and other Negro League players at least a chance to play in the Major Leagues. What an electric scene it would have been to see "Mules" Suttles approaching home plate in a St. Louis Cardinals' or Brooklyn Dodgers' uniform with the sound of fans screaming "Kick Mule, Kick!"

CHAPTER 12

Raymond Brown

The question of whether or not many Negro League players could have been successful in the Major Leagues is moot. Since black players before Jackie Robinson were not even given the opportunity to fail with Major League clubs the answer to the question is only left to speculation. Despite all that happened in barnstorming exhibition games or in winter league play the Major

League story of such black players as Raymond Brown and others, who had exceptional baseball talent, can never be completely told. Racial discrimination prevented it from being known.

While in the middle of the 1938 National League pennant race, the Pittsburgh Pirates received a telegraph wire from the local Negro newspaper, the Pittsburgh Courier. In the wire the newspaper's sportswriters suggested the Pirates could finish on top if they signed five Major League caliber players from Pittsburgh's two Negro League teams. The best Pirates' players, Paul "Big Poison" Waner and Lloyd "Little Poison" Waner, were both over 30 in the declining years of their careers. There were no exceptional arms on the team's pitching staff. The Pirates ignored the black sportswriters' suggestion sticking with the racial discrimination that kept black ballplayers out of the Major Leagues at that time.

Pittsburgh came up short, finishing second only two games behind the pennant winning Chicago Cubs. Surely, winning their first pennant in 11 years would have been worth taking a chance on the African American players. The Courier's sportswriters suggested Satchel Paige and "Cool Papa" Bell, who had both played with the Pittsburgh Crawfords in 1937. Additionally named in the telegraph were the Homestead Grays' Josh Gibson, Buck Leonard, and the team's ace pitcher, Raymond Brown. It is only speculation, but if these players were signed and had been at least moderately successful, the Pirates could have won two more games to capture the pennant that season.

Of the five players the sportswriters suggested to the Pirates, Brown has received the least notoriety in his career. Like other Negro League hurlers, Raymond Brown's abilities on the mound were overshadowed by the great Satchel Paige. The most famous pitcher in Negro League baseball during the 1930s and 1940s, Paige's accomplishments and showmanship antics on the mound were well known. Articles on him appeared not only in Negro newspapers, but also in large national ones that seldom carried anything about black baseball. Because of their refusal to cover the Negro Leagues, those newspapers missed heralding that no Negro

League pitcher won more than Raymond Brown. When Brown pitched the Homestead Grays knew they had a great chance for victory. If he had possessed some of Paige's talent for showmanship on the mound, Brown would have received more of Satchel's fame.

A versatile athlete, Brown made his debut into the world in Algers, Ohio on February 22 or 23, 1908. Located in western Ohio, the town is half the distance between Toledo and Dayton. He used his 6'1", 195 pound frame to become an all-state basketball center in high school. But that did not distract him from playing the game he loved - baseball. Brown could not only pitch, but he swung a solid bat. Early in his career he played outfield on days he had not been scheduled to pitch. The switch hitter also frequently pinch hit.

When facing Raymond Brown an opposing batter knew he would see a variety of pitches all difficult to make solid contact. Brown had a live fast ball to go along with a slider and a sinker. Later in his career he added a knuckle ball to his pitching arsenal. However, whenever in a tight situation, he used his best pitch; a curveball. With the game on the line and needing to get a batter out, Brown would confidently throw his curveball to get the job done. Even if batters guessed correctly and expected the pitch, they still struggled to hit it. Also known for his durability, Brown pitched 21 years in professional baseball with few serious arm problems.

He began playing Negro League baseball in 1930 with the Dayton Marcos. He played on the team while either working as a laborer or a student at Wilberforce College in Xenia, Ohio, which was near Dayton. The information as to which is contrasting. The Marcos had been a charter member of the NNL, but was not affiliated with any league by 1930. The next season, Brown played with the Indianapolis ABCs and in 1932 with the Detroit Wolves, a team in the ill-fated East-West League. Cum Posey owned both the Wolves and the Homestead Grays, who were not affiliated with any league that year. Along with Brown, Posey switched playing Willie Wells, "Cool Papa" Bell, Judy Johnson and others, between his two teams. When the East-West league closed down before the season ended, all played solely for the Grays. Raymond Brown established himself as one of Negro League baseball's pitchers in his years with the Homestead Grays.

With Brown as their ace pitcher, the Grays became one of the most dominant franchises in Negro League baseball. From 1937 – 1945 the team finished first place in the NNL nine times and played in four Negro League World Series, winning two: 1943 and 1944. Hall of Famers Josh Gibson and Buck Leonard led the Grays' power packed line up during those winning seasons. The 1943 team, which included "Cool Papa" Bell and Jud "Boojum" Wilson, is considered by some fans as one of the best in Negro League history. Brown's ties to the team went beyond just being its pitching ace. He married team owner Cum Posey's daughter in 1935.

Even with all of the offensive firepower demonstrated by the Grays, the pitching of Raymond Brown should not be undervalued or overlooked as a contributor to the team's success. With Brown on the mound, opposing teams knew they had to play almost a perfect game. Knowing it would be difficult scoring runs on him, those teams had to shut down the Grays' power filled line up to win. That did not happen very often. According to available game statistics and game recaps from black newspapers, Brown had a .742 Negro National League (NNL) winning percentage with the Grays. At one time he had a 27 game winning streak, including non-league (barnstorming) games. In his Negro League World Series action Brown won three games; including a one-hit shutout of the Birmingham Barons in 1943.

Negro League fans appreciated Brown more as part of those good Grays' teams than for his individual mound skills. They elected him to play in the East-West All Star Game only two times; 1935 (the starting pitcher for the East squad) and 1940.

Like most other Negro Leaguers, Brown played against white Major League and semi-professional players in fall exhibition and winter league games. In the late 1930s playing in the Cuban Winter League, he supposedly pitched both ends of a doubleheader, pitching 10 shutout innings in the first game before losing 1-0 in the eleventh and then pitched a five hit shutout in the night cap. This happened after he'd already pitched a no hitter the previous outing prior to the doubleheader. Cuban baseball fans called Brown

"Jabao", the Cuban name for light skinned black men. There is also some reference to a no hitter he pitched against the New York Yankees in the late 1940s while playing in Puerto Rico.

There is no certainty Raymond Brown could have duplicated this in the Major Leagues, but it shows he had enough potential to deserve a chance. His 12 years with the Grays coincided with the careers of Dizzy Dean, Carl Hubbell, and Bob Feller. But Brown could not pitch in the Major Leagues with them even though they were contemporaries.

Despite his winning Grays' seasons, Brown status as the owner's son-in-law caused problems with teammates. Many players believed he got favorable treatment from Cum Posey. A heavy drinker, Brown could be moody and constantly lost his temper. But his abilities on the field made his sometimes difficult behavior tolerable for Grays' managers.

By the mid-1940s, the Grays were in decline. The nucleus of the team, including Brown, was well over 30 years old. It had become an "old team" compared to others in the NNL and could not do on the diamond what it had done years before. The evidence of the team's decline was clear when it lost the 1945 Negro League World Series to the Cleveland Buckeyes four games to none. Brown lost Game Four 5 – 0. Then in the spring of 1946 team owner Cum Posey died, which added to the team's problems. Although Cum's brother Seward took over, the long-time core of Grays dismantled. Jud Wilson retired, Josh Gibson was sick and would die before the 1947 season, and others were released or traded. Only Buck Leonard and Sam Bankhead remained.

Despite experiencing soreness in his pitching arm for the first time, Raymond Brown signed to play in the Mexican League in 1946. It would be the first time in 13 years he would not wear a Homestead Grays' uniform.

Formed in the 1930s by Mexican shipping magnate Jorge Pasqual, the Mexican League had a reputation of successfully luring players away from Negro League baseball. Satchel Paige, Josh Gibson, Roy Campanella, Ray Dandridge, and others all played in Mexico during their baseball careers. The teams in the league offered the black players more money than the Negro League teams. Also, and even more important, the players did not encounter the racial prejudice they faced in the United States.

Considered the "backbone" of the league by Mexican sportswriters, black players were enthusiastically embraced and highly celebrated by the baseball fans in Mexico. In 1946 Pasquel lured Max Lanier, Sal Maglie, Mickey Owen, and nine other Major League players to the Mexican League by promises of higher salaries. Recovered from his sore arm, Brown pitched for the teams in Tampico and Monterrey.

The wall of racial prejudice in baseball crumbled in 1947 when Jackie Robinson began playing for the Brooklyn Dodgers. Slowly, more opportunities to play in the Major Leagues began opening for African Americans. However, the wall came down too late for former Negro Leaguers like Raymond Brown. Close to 40 years old, he did not even get to pitch in a big league team's minor league system as did his former teammate with the Homestead Grays, Roy Partlow, and a few other older pitchers from black teams.

After three seasons in the Mexican League (1946 -1949), Brown went to Quebec, Canada to pitch in the Provincial League. Canada's most established independent summer league had been welcoming black players since the 1920s. There were other former Negro Leaguers playing there in 1950. In addition, those Major League players serving a five year suspension for jumping to the Mexican League in 1946 were also in Canada that year. Pitching for Quebec, the forty two year old Brown proved his curveball could still get hitters out as he helped the team make the playoffs. The next year Brown's team won the league championship.

In the fall of 1950 the Homestead Grays took the field for the last time before their home fans in Washington, DC. It had been ten years since the Grays began playing half their home games in Washington, soon abandoning Pittsburgh altogether to become the nation capital's black team. On the verge of financially collapsing, the Grays would disband by the end of the year. But on this day, they were playing a doubleheader against the Philadelphia Stars who sent out Satchel Paige to pitch the first game. The Grays' fans had seen their team and Paige battle many times in the past. For the team's last appearance before their fans it was only fitting they face an old foe. Also, it was only fitting that the Grays would send to the mound their former ace, Raymond Brown. Finished with his season in Canada, Brown signed on to pitch for the Grays for that one day. He had not put on a Grays' uniform since 1945. Brown did that day as he had done his entire career with the team, pitch winning baseball. The Grays beat Satchel Paige and the Stars 7 – 1. They also won the second game, ending the team's history in Washington on a winning note.

Brown spent the final two years of his baseball career, 1952 and 1953, pitching for teams in a Canada semi-pro independent league. In his last year he was 13 – 5 and his team won the league championship. Brown remained in Canada for a while after retiring from baseball before returning to Dayton where he died in 1965.

Raymond Brown's 2006 induction into the National Baseball Hall of Fame gives him a new identity. More than the ace pitcher for the Homestead Grays during the team's most successful years and more than another good Negro League pitcher overshadowed by the legendary Satchel Paige, Brown's Hall of Fame selection recognizes him as a true champion. When he pitched, his teams won. In almost every league he played during his baseball career Brown pitched his team to a championship.

CHAPTER 13

Willard Brown

The Kansas City Monarchs conducted spring training in Shreveport, Louisiana for a number of years. Many of the African American boys growing up in the western Louisiana city dreamed of playing baseball with the team from Kansas City, one of the most successful franchises in the Negro Leagues. As the boys watched their heroes on the practice field they visualized of one day wearing a Monarchs' uniform. In 1929 fourteen year old Willard Jessie Brown served as the Monarchs' batboy during spring training. Six years later, the dream of many African American boys in Shreveport became a reality for Willard Brown.

Born June 26, 1915 in Shreveport, Brown first played with a black minor league team in Monroe, Louisiana. It was there in 1934 that the nineteen year old player caught the eye of Monarchs' owner J. L. Wilkinson. The raw talent and potential made quite an impression on the long time baseball man. Brown made $10 a week playing for that minor league team and did not hesitate to accept the $250 bonus and $125 monthly salary offered to be a Monarch. Wilkinson signed him as a shortstop and pitcher. Although he believed the young player would be outstanding, the Monarchs' owner did not realize his team's former batboy would become a Hall of Famer.

Based on the available box scores, game summaries from the sports page archives of black newspapers, and other written or verbal information; no one other than Josh Gibson hit more Negro League home runs than Willard Brown. The top home run hitter in the Negro American League (NAL) from the late 1930s through the 1940s, Brown at home plate with a bat created fear in the eyes of pitchers more than any other power hitter during that period.

His family and friends called him "Willie". But Josh Gibson gave him the nickname "Home Run" because every time their teams played Brown outslugged him. The name stuck and Brown lived up to it by hitting many tape measure home runs. After seeing a Brown home run in Philadelphia's Shibe Park Philadelphia Tribune sportswriter Rollo Wilson said he had seen no one other than Babe Ruth hit a longer one in that stadium.

Few players in the Negro Leagues or Major Leagues possessed Willard "Home Run" Brown's combination of skills. A true power hitting slugger, Brown is credited for winning seven NAL home run titles. But Brown had the batting stroke to also hit for a high average. He is given credit for winning three NAL batting titles and finishing second twice. In addition, Brown ran with blazing speed. He started with the Monarchs as a shortstop, but moved to the outfield where his speed could be put to better use. No one could run down balls which appeared beyond an outfielder's reach like "Home Run" Brown. Catchers hated to see him on the base paths. He ran so fast he stole bases standing up. He did not need to slide to beat their throws.

At 5'11", 195 pounds Willard Brown did not have the typical build of a powerful slugger. But he had surprising physical strength. He used a forty ounce bat which was too heavy for most hitters to swing at pitches. When asked how he could swing such a heavy bat, Brown said, "I do not swing it, I just lay it on the ball."

It is scary to think what Brown, the classic example of a "bad ball" hitter, could have done if he had been more disciplined at the plate. It did not have to be a strike, if he liked the pitch he swung. Brown supposedly hit a home run off a pitch that bounced in the dirt. Pitchers could not use Brown's impatience as a hitter to get him out. They tried, but it only made "Home Run" Brown a more dangerous hitter. Trying to get him to chase a pitch out of the strike zone many times resulted in giving what he wanted, a pitch to hit.

Although no one ever questioned Willard Brown's baseball talent, he did receive some criticism at times for a perceived lack of motivation and hustle. His laid back, easy going manner left some with the impression Brown did not give his best effort at times. Some teammates claimed he only hustled when playing in front of large crowds, like the Sunday doubleheaders the Monarchs played. They also called Brown "Sonny" because he was reluctant to play in imperfect weather. On cool cloudy or rainy days he would take to the bench. On beautiful sunny days when in front of large crowds, the fans would see the best of Willard Brown.

Brown had a tendency to appear bored during games. When that happened it is said he would take a magazine with him to the outfield to read between pitches. And sometimes he would walk instead of running to his outfield position, holding up the start of an inning. This gave an impression of Brown by some as having a "prima donna" attitude.

But former teammate and manager Buck O'Neil said, "Willard was so talented, he did not look as if he was hustling. Everything looked so easy for him." Brown's extreme talent made it appear he did things effortlessly. While most players ran around the bases, he seemed to glide. The exhaustion of the game would be evident on most players, but it appeared Brown hardly broke a sweat. O'Neil felt that no matter what "Home Run" Brown did, people thought he could do a little more because of his enormous talent.

But Negro League fans appreciated the play of Willard Brown. They selected him to participate in six Negro League East-West All Star Games. In ten All Star plate appearances Brown had five hits.

As an indication of Negro League baseball's relative prosperity after surviving the economic depression of the late 1920s and 1930s, the Negro League World Series was played in 1942. There had not been one since 1927. The 1942 fall classic saw the two most recognized Negro League franchises tangle, the Kansas City Monarchs against the Homestead Grays. Willard Brown was one of the series' hitting stars as the Monarchs swept the Grays four games to none. He batted .412 (7 hits in 17 at bats) with one double, one triple, and of course one home run.

Like many other black and white professional baseball players in the 1940s Brown served in the Army during World War II. His unit, part of the Quartermaster Corps, came ashore on Normandy Beach during the historic June 6, 1944 "D-Day" invasion of German occupied France by Allied forces. Serving in the military cost Brown two years of his baseball career. However, while serving, he along with Newark Eagles' pitcher Leon Day played with one of the first integrated military sports team. After the war ended in 1945, the Army used baseball to help occupy the troops in Europe before they were transported home. Brown's team won a best three out of five series against General Patton's squad made up of Major League players in the Army. Legend has it Brown hit two home runs in the series.

After returning from the military, Brown helped the Kansas City Monarchs win another NAL pennant in 1946. He showed no negative effects of missing two seasons, once again leading the NAL in home runs. However, the team lost the Negro League World Series to the Newark Eagles.

In 1947 Brown played an overlooked part of a major event in baseball history. He along with four other African Americans crossed over the "invisible color line" to integrate the Major Leagues. By being in the opening day lineup for the Brooklyn Dodgers to start the 1947 National League season, Jackie Robinson became the first African American to play Major League baseball since before the beginning of the 20th Century. On July 5, 1947, Larry Doby of the Newark Eagles made his debut with the Cleveland Indians and became the first African American to play in Major League Baseball's American League. Two weeks later "Home Run" Brown and his Monarch teammate Henry Thompson were signed by the St. Louis Browns. Needing more help on the mound for the pennant race, the Dodgers in late August signed African American pitcher Dan Bankhead. Of those historic African American breakthroughs, Robinson's is the one in which books have been written and movies produced. Brown and Thompson's role in the breakthrough is overlooked because of the St. Louis Browns' lack of true commitment to integrate Major League baseball at that time.

At the time he signed, Brown led the NAL in batting average; an indication his skills had not faded even in his mid to late 30s. But the St. Louis Browns were in last place, the worst team in the American League. During home games they played in front of less than 1,000 fans on average. Unlike the Dodgers and Indians, the team had no long term interest in developing African American players. It saw the signing of Brown and Thompson as a quick way of generating fan interest to boost game attendance.

After joining the St. Louis team, "Home Run" Brown and Thompson faced the same type of racist attitudes and actions confronted by Jackie Robinson. They received a cold reception from white teammates, many verbally expressing displeasure against black players. Brown and Thompson had to also endure racial insults from some opponents and fans while on the field. "Home Run" deserved the opportunity to play in the Major Leagues. He had exhibited the skills in Negro League baseball to be given the chance to make it. None of the Browns' starting outfielders were hitting over .250. But "Home Run" Brown did not get a fair chance to show what he could do.

Despite the unspectacular performances of the other outfielders that season, team manager Muddy Ruel decided to use Brown sparingly without giving an explanation. "Home Run" first debuted on July 20th as the Browns became the first Major League team to field two black players. On July 23rd Brown got four hits against the New York Yankees in Yankee Stadium. On August 13 he hit an inside the park home run against Hall of Fame pitcher Hal Newhouser of the Detroit Tigers, the first American League home run hit by an African American player.

Brown's stay in the Major Leagues did not last long. Having two black players on the team did not increase fan interest and boost game attendance as the Browns had hoped. Also, the team did not want to pay a full season's salary to them. On August 23, "Home Run" Brown and Thompson were released; obviously not given a fair opportunity to showcase their skills. In 27 games, playing mainly at second base, Hank Thompson hit .256, only .005 less than the Browns' primary second baseman John Berardino who became a TV actor after leaving baseball. While with the St. Louis team "Home Run" Brown only hit .179. Not playing every day as when with the Monarchs, he did not have a chance to get into a comfortable "grove" while batting.

He did not have a period of adjustment to be prepared for the pressure of being one of the first black players in a previously all white league. The Dodgers prepared Jackie Robinson by having him play a year with their top minor league team. But Brown and Thompson went straight from the Monarchs to Browns and were not given time to prepare for what they would face. Larry Doby came straight to the Indians from the Negro Leagues and hit only .156 in 1947. However, the Indians did not release him. They helped him develop during spring training in 1948 and he became the team's centerfielder for the next eight years. Bankhead had a poor season with the Dodgers after coming straight to them from the Negro American League's Memphis Red Sox. The team, however, did not give up on him. He pitched in the Dodgers' minor league system and in 1950 was a part of the team's Major League starting rotation.

Coming from the Monarchs, Brown had played his entire career with an organization that had a tradition of winning. This made it hard mentally for him to accept the long standing losing attitude of the Brown's. He said, "The Browns could not beat the Monarchs no kind of way, only if we was asleep. That's the truth. They didn't have nothing. Major League team? They got to be kidding."

If his distastefully brief experience in the Major Leagues left him angry and bitter about baseball, "Home Run" Brown did not let it show in his play on the diamond. After returning to the Monarchs, he continued hitting over .300 the reminder of the season. Later that year in the Puerto Rican Winter League, a sixty game season, he won the Triple Crown, hitting more home runs than any player had ever hit during a season in Puerto Rico. His record of 27 home runs that season still remains unbroken. He also won the Puerto Rican Winter League Triple Crown during the 1949 – 1950 winter season. The baseball fans there called Brown "Ese Hombre", which means "That Man". As he came up to bat, they would lovingly shout, "Here comes that man again." In 1991 Brown was in the first class inducted into the Puerto Rican Baseball Hall of Fame.

As the decade of the 1940s ended, Brown found himself too old (35 years old) to get another Major League opportunity and he faced the quickly declining future of Negro League baseball. He had been with the Monarchs since 1935, his tenure with the team only interrupted by playing part of the 1940 season in the Mexican League, military service in 1944 and 1945, and his brief time with the St. Louis Browns in 1947. With the face of baseball changing, Brown did not return to the team for the 1950 season.

Over the final last years of his baseball career, Brown played in the minor leagues, except for a one season return to the Monarchs in 1951. Along with Dave Hoskins, Bill Greason, and a few others, he was one of the former Negro League players that integrated the Texas League (Double AA baseball) in the 1950s. "Home Run" Brown hit 23 home runs in 1953 and 35 home runs in 1954 for the Dallas Eagles. He hit 19 home runs in 1955 for the Houston Buffalos and 14 home runs in 1956 for the Tulsa Oilers; his last season in the Texas League. During the Puerto Rican Winter League in 1957 Brown made his last appearance in professional baseball and hit his last two home runs.

Willard "Home Run" Brown died in Houston, Texas while suffering from Alzheimer's disease on August 4, 1996. There is the unanswered question of how successful he could have been in the Major Leagues had he been given another opportunity following his brief stay with the St. Louis Browns in 1947. Hank Thompson, Brown's Monarchs teammate who went with him to St. Louis, got another opportunity. After being released by the Browns, he signed with the New York Giants in 1949 and played in the Major Leagues for eight years. Brown never received another chance.

There is a belief that if given another opportunity Willard Brown still would not have made it in the Major Leagues. Everyone knew he had the talent, but many believed he did not have the right attitude. They say his easy going laid back style of play would have caused problems with Major League managers. Brown would have had to change his approach to his game. At his age, over thirty, many believed it would have been hard for him to do.

But Willard "Home Run" Brown's induction into the Baseball Hall of Fame in 2006 is not based on what he may have been able to do. It is based on what he did. And what he did was become one of the greatest home run hitters in Negro League baseball.

PROFILES – TEAM OWNERS

Chapter 14

Sol White

Sol White's "History of Colored Baseball" gives an account of African American ballplayers in the beginning times of professional baseball. The book covers the earliest years of organized baseball, late 19th Century through early 20th, and gives a vivid picture of the obstacles black professional baseball players faced as the game began its journey to becoming the "National Pastime". These were the obstacles that King Solomon "Sol" White himself experienced and overcame as a ballplayer, manager, coach, and sportswriter. He was a true pioneer of the game he loved.

Born on June 12, 1868, Sol White began his baseball career first as a talented infielder for an integrated, amateur team in his hometown of Bellaire, Ohio. White was a speedster who played each infield and outfield position with flair.

During the major portion of his playing career, late 1880s and 1890s, White experienced the rough landscape for black ballplayers. Although "the invisible color line" keeping black players out professional baseball had not yet been drawn, the hostile attitude directed towards them showed they were not welcomed. The small number of African Americans trying to play in the developing professional leagues had to endure anger, racial taunts, verbal abuse, and threats of bodily harm from teammates, opponents, and fans. African American players also had to face the uncertain financial realities of black teams. This resulted in many of the players moving each season from one team to another. There is indication Sol White played in this type of baseball environment while attending college either in the late 1880s or mid-1890s at Wilberforce University (Xenia, Ohio).

Although only 18 years old, White started first professionally in 1886 with Wheeling (West Virginia) of the Ohio States League and hit over .300 in a little over 50 games. As the rancor over African Americans playing on white teams continue to get louder, White thought he had found a less combustible situation the next season by playing with the Pittsburgh Keystones. The Keystones were a black team in what attempted to be an organized league for black players, the National Colored Base Ball League. White played second base and hit over .300, but the league went out of business after four weeks and he went back to the white team in Wheeling.

The color line became more solid with less fewer breaks in it during the 1890s. White was back with the Pittsburgh Keystones in 1888, but it was no longer considered a professional team. However, the other black professional teams the Keystones occasionally played against noticed that White was a talented player and he played for one of them in 1889; the New York Gorhams. Although it had the New York City name, the team represented the city of Easton, Pennsylvania in the Middle States League. It was one of the disappearing breaks in the color line. The Cuban Giants, organized in 1885 and considered by many historians the first African American pro baseball team, won the league championship that year representing Trenton, New Jersey.

In 1890 Sol White played for the Monarchs of York, Pennsylvania. The team's owner, J. Monroe Kreiter, had also attracted many of the players from the previous year's Cuban Giants. Failing in their attempt to get higher salaries from the Giants' owner, John M. Bright, the players were easily lured away by the money that Kreiter offered. The Monarchs represented the city of York in the Eastern Interstate League. It would be one of the last breaks in the color line.

White played briefly in 1895 with Fort Wayne, Indiana of the Western Interstate League. It would be the last time he played on an integrated team. As the 1890s came to a close there were no black players in organized white baseball. The 'invisible color line" had been set and would stay intact for over 40 years.

With the door to Major League professional baseball closed for African American players, Sol White continued his career in the 1890s with teams that were a part of Negro League baseball's early beginnings. They were African American teams that played small town white semi-pro teams, other black teams, and anyone that wanted to play them. No official Negro League existed at that time. He played for the Cuban Giants in 1893 – 1894, the Page Fence Giants in 1895, the Cuban X Giants in 1896 – 1899, and the Chicago Columbia Giants in 1900. All of which were top African American professional teams of that period.

In 1902 White joined forces with white sportswriter H. Walter Schlichter to start a new black team, the Philadelphia Giants. As co-owner, team manager, and one of the team's top players, White built what some called one of the best black teams of the new century's first ten years. Some of the best black players of that time such as Frank Grant, Pete Hill, Charlie Grant, Grant "Home Run"

Johnson, and Rube Foster played for the Giants at some point when White headed the team. Unofficial records show the team won 134 games in 1905. They were challenged by the Cuban X Giants at the end of the season to a best of two out of three series. White's Giants won the series and proclaimed themselves Negro baseball champions.

After the 1906 season Rube Foster complained the Giants ballplayers' salaries needed to be raised. When no action from White followed, Foster left to become the player/manager of the Chicago Leland Giants and he took many of White's best players by offering them more money. But the departure of Foster and others did not shake up the Philadelphia Giants. White found other good ballplayers and continued to have an excellent team. In 1908 White accepted a challenge from Foster to play an after season series. Although not officially called a "World Series" the contest pitted for the first time the best black team in the east (Philadelphia Giants) against the best in the west (Chicago Leland Giants) in a post season series. It ended with each team winning three games. It is still unknown after all these years as to why the teams did not play a game seven to determine a champion.

Due to a financial disagreement with Schlichter, White left the team after the 1909 season. Even though Schlichter's company had published White's book, the two men could not resolve their dispute. The Philadelphia Giants were never the same after White's departure. With him no longer there to guide it the team faded away and was never organized again.

But Sol White did not fade away after leaving Philadelphia. In 1910 he managed the Brooklyn Royal Giants. The next year he was given another opportunity to start a new team as he had done in Philadelphia. When New York sports promoter Jess McMahon started his New York Lincoln Giants in 1911 he knew who to get for assembling and managing the team, Sol White. With this new opportunity White once again put together one of the best teams in Negro League baseball. John Henry "Pop" Lloyd, "Cannonball" Dick Redding, "Smokey" Joe Williams, and Louis Santop were players on the first Lincoln Giants team White assembled. The Lincoln Giants were the first team to entertain the fans by doing baseball stunts and skill exhibitions before the game. Although not documented, it is said the team won over 100 games that year. However, White did not have an opportunity to share in the team's success. McMahon replaced him at mid-season because they had a disagreement. White's impact as the team's organizer and first manager remained after he left. The Lincoln Giants were the top team in Negro League baseball for the following two years.

After staying out of the game for a while when he left the Lincoln Giants, Sol White resurfaced at a very important time for Negro League baseball. In 1920 White's former player Rube Foster started the Negro National League (NNL). With it being the most ambitious effort at that time to have a professional baseball league for black players it is no surprise White got involved. In the league's second year White became coach and advisor for a new team, the Columbus Buckeyes. Managed by White's former player "Pop" Lloyd, the team had a bad year finishing next to last and dropped out of the league. White managed another new NNL team in 1924, the Cleveland Browns. It had a 17 – 34 record and only lasted that one season.

After finishing his career on the baseball diamond White remained involved in the game as a sportswriter. His articles about Negro League baseball appeared in newspapers such as the New York Amsterdam, Cleveland Advocate, and Pittsburgh Courier. The articles were avenues for him to express his strong support of black ballplayers and the Negro Leagues.

Considered a "true gentleman" of the game by all who knew him, there are no wild and crazy stories, true or mythical about Sol White. He believed black ballplayers needed to have a serious approach to play baseball. White felt they were still professional players even though racial discrimination kept them out of the Major Leagues and they should act professional. That was the message Sol White preached to black ballplayers no matter his role: as a player, manager, or sportswriter. This made him a bright light for Negro League baseball for more than fifty years.

White hoped that the day would come when African Americans

played in the Major Leagues. He said, "There are grounds for hoping someday the bar will drop and some good man will be chosen from out of the colored profession that will be a credit to all, and pave the way for others to follow." White lived to see this hope become a reality when Jackie Robinson took the field in a Brooklyn Dodger's uniform on April 15, 1947. White, 79 years old at the time lived in Harlem, only a subway trip to Ebbets Field in Brooklyn where Robinson played. There is no indication White attended the game in person, but surely its importance did not escape his attention. That game began the reality of White's hope, the coming to life of the words he spoke.

Sol White died on August 26, 1955.

CHAPTER 15

James L. Wilkinson

For nearly all the first half of the 20th Century J.L. Wilkinson looked at players differently than by the racial prejudice that existed in professional baseball during the period. Despite being white, he judged a baseball player according to ability not skin color. He knew African American and Hispanic ballplayers were talented and treated them with dignity and respect. One of the teams he organized, All Nations, had a mixture of players from different races, nationalities, and cultures. Wilkinson also owned the Kansas City Monarchs, one of the most successful and celebrated franchises in Negro League baseball.

"Loyal", "fair", "trustworthy", and "generous" were words used by former players to describe the man they playfully called "Wilkie". His relationship with African American and Hispanic players was a rare example of racial togetherness in professional baseball long before Jackie Robinson and integration. It showed Wilkinson to be a man ahead of his time.

Born the son of a college professor on May 14, 1878 in Algona, Iowa, Wilkinson showed the potential of being a good pitcher in his youth. But an injury put an end to his career as a player and changed him to look at the game he loved as entertainment for fans.

He first organized a girl's baseball team in 1909 that traveled throughout Iowa and surrounding states by train in a Pullman railroad car. In addition to playing the game, it had an orchestra that gave fans a concert and one of the team's few male players would have a wrestling match with a challenger from the grandstand. From the beginning Wilkinson did not fear doing the unusual to make the games entertaining for the fans.

In 1912 he put together a racially mixed team called All Nations. No one had seen a team like it in baseball at that time, with black, white, Native American, Hispanic, and ballplayers of other different nationalities and ethnic groups together wearing the same uniform. They played against the best white semipro teams in towns throughout the country's heartland to the Pacific coast and traveled in a private railroad car. A group of wrestlers and a band travelled with the team to give more entertainment to fans attending the games. But the All Nations' players were not entertainers, they were professional ballplayers.

In 1915 he moved the team from Des Moines, Iowa to Kansas City and after World War I added Jose Mendez, John Donaldson, and Cristobal Torriente; all Major League caliber players to the roster. The next year the team won games against the Chicago American Giants and Indianapolis ABCs. A sportswriter for the Chicago

Defender, a leading black newspaper, called All Nations "the best example of how black and white teammates can successfully play together." What Wilkinson did with his team did not change anything. African American and Hispanic players would be kept out of the Major Leagues for over another 30 years.

The brainchild of Andrew "Rube" Foster, the Negro National League (NNL) became the first official black professional league at a 1920 meeting in Kansas City. Wilkinson played a part in this ground breaking venture. Although Foster did not initially want any white owners in the league, Wilkinson came to the meeting with a lease agreement for the Kansas City stadium his team would use. He had the support of Kansas City's black community through the relationship developed within it since moving to town with his All Nations team. Wilkinson and Foster's relationship grew to one of mutual respect and trust. JL became the NNL's Secretary and was one of its most influential team owners.

Although originally called the Browns, Wilkinson's new team took the name of a previous all black team in Kansas City, the Kansas City Monarchs. For this new team Wilkinson chose the best players from All Nations and added others such as Wilber "Bullet" Rogan, Lemuel Hawkins, and Dobie Moore, all three coming out of the Army. Wilkinson kept his younger players on All Nations to develop and season them so they would be prepared for the Monarchs. It would be more than 10 years later before Major League teams would create a similar minor league development system. This showed that his view of the sport was far ahead of other owners. Operating his team in a way that gained the respect of other league owners, Wilkinson's Monarchs were considered a first class organization. Hilldale Club owner Ed Bolden called Wilkinson "the most fair minded, square shooting white man I have ever met who is interested in Negro baseball."

The Monarchs won NNL pennants in 1923, 1924, 1926, and 1929. They played Bolden's team, the Eastern Colored League's champion, in the first two Negro League World Series championships. Kansas City won in 1924, while Hilldale won the next year.

After the 1930 season Wilkinson pulled the Monarchs out of the NNL. The "Great Depression" that had begun in 1929 caused economic problems for Negro League teams. Game attendance declined, fans no longer had the luxury to afford tickets, team revenues shrunk. The ECL had gone out of business two seasons earlier and many NNL teams would be gone by the 1931 season. In addition, league founder and its pillar of strength Rube Foster died in 1930 after suffering mental and physical illness. Looking at the difficult economic challenges that faced black professional baseball, Wilkinson believed it would be more profitable for the Monarchs to play the small town circuit. A big deal for the townspeople, they would fill the grandstands to see their local semipro team play the famous Kansas City Monarchs. No longer tied into a league, Wilkinson's team could schedule more games to make more money. Being the first Negro League team to travel exclusively by bus, an 18 capacity one with reclining seats, the Monarchs took to the highway. The Kansas City Monarchs' bus travelled up and down the roads of the country's heartland between the Canadian and Mexican borders.

The Monarchs' roadshow fit perfectly with Wilkinson's idea that would change the game forever; night baseball. Until that time baseball games were played during the daytime. If the game did not end before dark it would be completed the next day. But Wilkinson believed playing games at night would give people who worked during the day an opportunity to attend, bringing more fans to the game and generating more revenue for his team.

Using his house as collateral, he borrowed money from his bank to purchase a portable lighting system that travelled with the Monarchs. Unlike the powerful lights used at today's baseball stadiums, these were on retractable poles transported on 6 trucks. Powered by a portable generator (Sterling Marine 100-kilowatt) ran by a loud gas engine (250 horsepower, six-cylinder, triple-carburetor), the system drew complaints about its noise from neighbors around the baseball fields in some towns. One story told is that officials in one town were upset because the system's engine noise disturbed the zoo animals. It took twelve men to install forty-four giant, non-glare floodlights that hung 50 feet high on the steel poles that were mounted on the beds of the trucks stationed around the field. Despite the noise the system succeeded as curious fans eagerly flocked to the baseball field to watch their team play the Monarchs under the lights. Major League teams would not be playing night games until 1936.

Wilkinson continued to keep the Monarchs operating through the economic depression of the 1930s. He made personal sacrifices in order to put money back into the team. Unlike some black professional teams during that time, he did not partner with numbers operators in order for the Monarchs to survive. Former Monarchs say "Wilkie" always had the money needed to pay their salaries. He never missed a team payroll, something few owners in the Negro League could claim.

In 1937 Wilkinson played a part in forming a third black league, the Negro American League (NAL). A reconstructed NNL had been started in 1933. Although the Monarchs were a part of the original NNL in the 1920s, Wilkinson initially did not want the team in the new league. However, he believed the economic climate had begun to change by 1937 and thought it beneficial to be in the newly formed NAL. Quickly, he became one of the most respected and influential owners in the new league and his team one of the league's best. By the time Wilkinson retired in 1948, the Monarchs had won six NAL pennants. When Negro League baseball reinstated its World Series in the 1940s, the Monarchs played in two. They defeated the legendary great Homestead Grays in the 1942 Series to be Negro League World Champions.

According to former Monarchs' first baseman and manager Buck O'Neil, "Wilkinson treated his players like his sons." This included standing up for them in the face of prejudice. Former Monarchs tell of the time the owner threatened to not play a game in Montana when he discovered the town's restaurant had refused to serve food to his players. He told the manager of his team's opponent to refund the fans' money, the Monarchs were not going to play. After being assured his players would be welcome in the restaurant, Wilkinson allowed his team to play the game.

The Monarch players were required by their owner to have a professional attitude about the game both on and off the field. Wilkinson allowed no gambling on the team bus or in the players' hotel rooms. The players could not wear their team jackets outside the ballpark. A suit or sport coat was the required dress. If a player needed help with his wardrobe the owner would send him to a tailor on 18th and Vine in Kansas City to be fitted at Wilkinson's expense.

He also did not hesitate to help players hurt or in the last stage of their careers. "Wilkie" would say, "They can still do some good. They've done a lot for the Negro Leagues and made us all money. So I am just trying to help them."

Wilkinson is the one who stepped in to save the career of the great Negro League pitcher Satchel Paige. In 1937 while playing in Mexico Paige hurt his pitching arm. Word got out that at 32 years old he had lost the zip on his pitches. No team expressed interest to sign him the next season. Paige feared he would never pitch again. But Wilkinson signed him to pitch for the Monarchs' touring team which travelled through the northwestern United States and Canada. Not a totally unselfish decision, the Monarchs' owner saw it as a potential opportunity to make money. He could visualize the baseball fans in those small towns running to the ballpark to see Satchel Paige, even though the legendary pitcher appeared to be on the decline. Cleverly Wilkinson named the team "The Satchel Paige All Stars". The team's appearances were big events for the small towns, even though Paige only pitched one or two innings each game.

Mysteriously by the middle of the 1938 season Paige's arm recovered and he slowly regained his all-star form. With his arm sound again Paige joined the Monarchs' main team in 1939 and helped them win NAL pennants in 1940 -1942. The clashes Paige had with the owners of the teams he pitched for during his career are part of Negro League baseball lore. But Satchel showed Wilkinson more respect and loyalty than he did other owners, always giving the Monarchs' owner credit for helping to revive his career.

Helping to build up and maintain Negro League baseball for more than two decades, J. L. Wilkinson also ironically played an initial role in what eventually led to its end. In 1945 he invited to the Monarchs' spring training camp a 26 year old former college football and basketball star that had been honorably discharged from the Army. Wilkinson saw the speed and the intense competitive nature the player exhibited on the baseball field. He saw something special in him. Wilkinson signed Jackie Roosevelt Robinson to play for the Monarchs.

Although not the best player on that year's team, Robinson soon caught the eye of Brooklyn Dodgers' General Manager Branch Rickey. Ignoring Robinson's contract with the Monarchs, on August 28, 1945 Rickey signed him to play for the Dodgers. Less than two years later on April 15, 1947, Robinson became the first African American to play Major League baseball since before the beginning of the 20th Century.

Like other Negro League club owners, Wilkinson had mixed emotions about Robinson's signing. He was happy to see the door finally open for black players to play in the Major Leagues, but concerned about what it meant for the future of Negro League baseball. He did not loudly complain that the Monarchs still had Robinson under contract and they had received no compensation from the Dodgers. But he knew that when more black players were chosen by Major League teams, it would spell the end of Negro League baseball. Twenty-seven former Kansas City Monarchs were signed by Major League teams, the most of any Negro League franchise. In addition to Jackie Robinson, that number includes other Major League All Star players Satchel Paige, Ernie Banks, Gene Baker, George Altman, and Elston Howard.

In 1948 at 70 years old and losing his eyesight, J. L. Wilkinson stepped away from baseball and the Negro Leagues. He sold his ownership share of the Monarchs to business partner Tom Baird, part owner of the team since the mid-1930s. After the Major League Philadelphia Athletics moved to Kansas City in 1955 and became the Kansas City Athletics, Baird sold the financially struggling Monarchs to an out of town buyer.

When he retired Wilkinson remained in Kansas City where he had created and maintained one of the most successful franchises in Negro League history. As his health continued to decline Wilkinson saw the decline of Negro League baseball. As more black players went into the Major Leagues the institution he helped build continued to fade away. Wilkinson died on August 21, 1964, the last year of any record showing the existence of the Monarchs.

James Leslie Wilkinson's induction into the National Baseball Hall of Fame in 2006 is more than just another acknowledgement of Negro League baseball's place in the history of our national pastime. It represents his deserved recognition as a baseball team owner whose thinking and attitude about the game were ahead of his time.

CHAPTER 16

Cumberland Posey

Although he did not become an engineer and build barges like his father, "Cum" Posey built and maintained a winning tradition matched by few other teams in Negro League baseball. A number of the greatest African American baseball players in the first half of the Twentieth Century were a part of Posey's winning tradition known as "the long Gray line". They wore the uniform of his

Homestead Grays. Buck Leonard and Raymond Brown, both members of the Baseball Hall of Fame, spent most of their entire Negro League careers with the Grays. Hall of Famers Josh Gibson, "Cool Papa" Bell, Oscar Charleston, Judy Johnson, "Smokey Joe" Williams, Jud Wilson, Martin Dihigo, Willie Wells, and Willie Foster all at one time or another played for the Grays; one of the most renown franchises in Negro League baseball.

After beginning as a young outfielder for the team Posey went on to be the Grays field manager and eventually its owner. For approximately 35 years until his death in 1946, the Grays were a part of Posey's life. A smart businessman and an excellent judge of baseball talent, he has a prominent place in Negro League baseball history as one of its most successful team owners and influential league spokespersons.

Homestead, Pennsylvania lies across the Monongahela River from Pittsburgh, the center of America's steel production as the country turned into the 20th Century. The people of Homestead lived under the smoke, steam, dirt, and grime of the Carnegie Steel Mill. Most of the residents were employed by the mill, including many African Americans who had migrated from southern states.

Homestead was the birthplace of Cumberland Willis Posey, Jr. on June 20, 1890. However, Posey's destiny would not be tied to steel. His parents were educated. His mother a teacher and his father was an entrepreneur. An engineer that built boats and operated a coal and ore business, Cum Sr. had the distinction of being possibly the richest African American in the area. In college Cum Jr. studied chemistry leaning towards becoming a pharmacist. But sports had such a hold of his heart he could not ignore it.

A star athlete at Homestead High School, Posey played football, basketball, and baseball as a teenager. Named Pittsburgh area's top high school basketball player in 1909, Posey (5'9", 140 pounds) also received national attention as one of the best guards in the country. He played college basketball at Penn State and Duquesne.

However, baseball was a more popular sport in Posey's hometown of Homestead. The black steel workers passionately played it every weekend from spring through fall. There were many sandlot baseball teams sponsored by Pittsburgh area steel mills and companies in the steel industry. These teams would be opponents for a Homestead black team organized in 1900 called the Blue Ribbons. The Blue Ribbons also played against local white semi-professional teams. By the time Posey began playing for the team in 1911, its name had been changed to the Murdock Grays. Shortly afterwards the team became the Homestead Grays.

Posey used the speed he exhibited on the basketball court to develop into a decent centerfielder in baseball. He still played local semi-professional basketball during the winter in his early years with the Grays. It was during his involvement with basketball that the skills Posey used when he owned and operated the Grays were first exhibited. Along with his brother Seward, he organized and operated a basketball team that was successful for many years in the black semi-professional circuit. He continued to operate the team for 14 years after he began playing with the Grays.

Posey's status with Grays steadily increased as he was the team captain in 1916, the field manager in 1917, and in 1918 was also handling many of the team's business operations. Finally, Posey and a local businessman (Charles Walker) bought the Grays in 1920.

As the new decade began, Posey began moving the Grays to be more than a sandlot team. He brought in talented players who did not work at the mills and paid them a salary. He scheduled more games against teams with professional quality talent; most were white semi-professional teams in the Pittsburgh area. As the support from Pittsburgh's African American community grew, the Grays began playing their games at Forbes Field, home of Pittsburgh's Major League team, the Pirates. The Grays became a top attraction travelling to towns in Pennsylvania, Ohio, and West Virginia playing against the best local talent at each stop.

Posey met the challenge of making enough money to keep his team operating year to year, a problem many black professional clubs could not overcome as many went out of business. He did not shy away from doing what he thought best to keep the Homestead Grays alive. He declined invitations for the Grays to be in the Negro

National League (NNL) formed in 1920 and the Eastern Colored League (ECL) formed in 1923. While in favor of developing black baseball, he believed being in a league would reduce the number of games the Grays played and limit the money his team could make. The Grays remained independent of both leagues most of the 1920s.

A fierce competitor on the field, Posey operated the Grays with the same intense spirit. Stern and authoritarian as a field manager, he had strict rules for the players to follow. As an owner Posey did not hesitate to steal players from other Negro League teams by offering higher salaries to play for the Grays. The other team owners raged at him for getting the best ballplayers that way. But he willingly did what he thought needed to be done to make the Grays a winning team year after year.

The "Great Depression" that began in 1929 severely damaged black professional baseball. Fan attendance declined causing game revenues to drop and forcing teams out of business. The ECL shut down in 1928 and the NNL after the 1931 season. But the economic trouble black professional baseball faced at first did not slow down Cum Posey and his Homestead Grays. He began the new decade with the best team he ever assembled. Josh Gibson, Oscar Charleston, Judy Johnson, and "Smoky" Joe Williams were all on that 1930 team. He considered the team even better in 1931 after adding Willie Foster, Jud "Boojum" Wilson, Ted Page, and Ted "Double Duty" Radcliffe.

However, after the NNL shut down no official professional league for African Americans was in operation. Contrary to his prior thinking, Posey believed black professional baseball could not survive without an official pro league. Evidence of the change in his thinking was 1929 when he had the Grays in the ill-fated American Negro League along with many former ECL teams. The league failed after one season. Posey took the initiative himself to organize a new black league in 1932, the East-West League. It had eight teams including his Grays and another team he owned, the Detroit Wolves. The league failed after three months. Posey's critics said his plans for the league were too ambitious for the economic hardships facing black baseball fans at that time.

As the country's economic condition worsened, Posey struggled to pay the salaries of his ballplayers in 1932. He also faced a major challenge from the new black team in Pittsburgh started by Gus Greenlee a night club/restaurant owner and numbers operator, the Pittsburgh Crawfords. He used a tactic Posey himself employed to steal players from other teams. Greenlee offered the Grays' best players more money than Posey could pay them. Josh Gibson, Oscar Charleston, and three other players took Greenlee's offer and signed with the Crawfords. Other players for the Grays also left for other teams.

Determined to not let his team die, Cum Posey formed a business partnership in 1934 with Rufus "Sonnyman" Jackson, Homestead's main black numbers operator. Posey operated the club while Jackson provided the financial backing. Many black sportswriters thought partnering with whom some called "black mobsters" hurt Negro League baseball's image with the fans. But Posey and the other black owners said financial backing from those men did not influence the teams' performance on the field. The numbers bosses were just fans who loved the game. The truth was that if it were not for their investment Negro professional baseball may not have survived.

Jackson's financial backing allowed Posey to step away from being the field manager and devote all his time to rebuilding the team. He brought on Buck Leonard in 1934 as the first step of putting together what would be the most dominate Negro League team in the late 1930s and 1940s. The next year the Grays joined the Negro National League (NNL). Despite Posey's rebuilding efforts, the team could not finish ahead of the Pittsburgh Crawfords. In 1937 Posey got Josh Gibson back in a trade with his crosstown rival. Part of the trade, as rumored, included "Sonnyman" Jackson paying off a gambling debt of the Crawfords' owner. By getting back Gibson, Posey had the final piece to add to Leonard and the other players he assembled to begin the Grays' winning tradition. Over the next nine years the Homestead Grays won eight Negro National League pennants and two Negro League World Series Championships.

Never shy about voicing his opinion, Posey frequently had disputes with other Negro League club owners. He had a sports column, "Pointed Paragraphs" (1931 – 1936) and "Posey Points" (1937 – 1945), in the Pittsburg Courier which was the black newspaper his father helped start. Other team owners were often angry about what Posey wrote in his column as he many times criticized black baseball. But they still respected him as a smart baseball man and Posey was chosen to hold the position of NNL Secretary in 1937.

Few baseball club owners had competitive fire and grit like Cum Posey. If he could get away with it, he would bend the rules to get his Grays a win. In the 1942 Negro League World Series, the Grays lost the first three games to the Kansas City Monarchs. Facing elimination, Posey took drastic action. The Grays line up for Game Four included three star players from the Newark Eagles and one from the Philadelphia Stars. The Grays won the game 4 -1, but after a strong protest from the Monarchs, the league officials voided the victory and banned the Grays from using players from other teams. The Monarchs won the next game to win the championship. The incident showed how far Cumberland Posey, Jr. would go to win.

By 1940 Posey began scheduling some of the Grays home games in Washington, DC. He believed his team could build a wider fan base because of a larger African American population in the area than was in Pittsburgh. The decision proved to be correct. Washington's black community embraced the team as its own. Soon many believed the Grays were the best professional baseball team in the nation's capital even better than Major League baseball's Washington Senators.

Having seen all the great players in Negro League baseball in his years owning the Grays, Posey knew black players were good enough to play on Major League teams if given a chance. But he feared if this happened Negro League teams would lose their best players. That is why he opposed the campaign of black sportswriters for getting African American players into the Major Leagues that occurred after World War II. Posey believed Negro League team owners needed to first develop a plan for survival before integration in baseball happened.

Cum Posey died of lung cancer on March 28, 1946 and never saw Jackie Robinson, Don Newcombe, Roy Campanella, and other Negro Leaguers playing in the Major Leagues. What he feared started to become a reality by the end of the 1940s, but he did not live to see it.

Posey's election into the Baseball Hall of Fame in 2006 gave recognition to his contributions to the reality that he feared. His efforts as a team owner helped to sustain Negro League baseball and gave a way for Robinson, Newcombe, Campanella, and other black players to show they deserved an opportunity to be in the Major Leagues. The opportunity that evidently came and that they were prepared to successfully seize due to their grooming in Negro League baseball.

CHAPTER 17

Effa Manley

The inscription on the gravestone of Effa Manley is, "She loved baseball" - a fitting description of the only female team executive in Negro League baseball. As a woman at the head of a professional baseball team, Mrs. Manley stood out in a male dominated business. All of her life Effa Manley had to face being seen as different by those around her. Never claimed by her white father and raised in Philadelphia's African American community by her white mother and black stepfather, young Effa stood out among her family and neighborhood friends due to her light skin complexion. When she became an adult, Effa Manley chose to be considered black and faced the racial prejudice and discrimination of the times.

Along with her husband, Abraham "Abe" Manley, she owned the Newark Eagles. Her husband financed the team while Mrs. Manley managed the day to day business operations. Former Newark Eagles and Hall of Fame outfielder Monte Irvin said of her, "She was unique, effervescent, and knowledgeable. She ran the whole business end of the team." Under Mrs. Manley's guidance the Newark Eagles were one of the most competitive teams in the Negro Leagues during the late 1930s and 1940s. Hall of Fame players Willie Wells, Ray Dandridge, Leon Day, Biz Mackey, "Mules" Suttles, Larry Doby, and former Major League star Don Newcombe were former Eagles. Irvin, Day, Doby, and Mackey played on the Eagles' team that won the 1946 Negro League World Series.

A fighter, Mrs. Manley boldly faced confrontation when necessary to keep her team operating. She fought to make her voice heard among the male Negro League team owners who believed professional baseball had no place for women. With her flamboyant style and baseball instincts Effa Manley left her footprint on Negro League history. She is the first and only woman to be honored with a plaque in the hallowed halls of Cooperstown.

Born Effa Banks in Philadelphia, there is conflicting information on the year of her birth. The date most given is March 27, 1900, expressed by Mrs. Manley, as opposed to March 27, 1897 indicated in a few documents. She moved to New York after high school and worked in the millinery industry, with women's hats. While considered white by New Yorkers, Effa continued to hold on to the black environment in which she was raised. Although she worked in New York department stores where few if any Negros were hired, Effa lived in Harlem. According to her own admission, it was in New York she developed her love for baseball. "Babe Ruth made a baseball fan of me. I used to go to Yankee Stadium just to see him bat," she said.

While attending the 1932 World Series she met her husband, Abraham Manley, who was also an avid baseball fan and at least 12 - 15 years her senior. Manley was a real estate investor and also supposedly ran one of the biggest illegal "numbers" game operations in Newark. The success of his endeavors would provide the funds for him and his wife's entry into Negro League baseball. They married in 1935. He was the second of four husbands Effa would have in her lifetime.

In that same year they formed a Negro League team in Brooklyn called the "Eagles". Mrs. Manley said the name came from her husband's hopes that "they would fly high." From the very beginning as baseball team owners, the Manleys had a clearly defined partnership, one she described as perfect. Abe provided the money and despite having no prior financial experience, Effa took an active role as co-owner by handling the day to day operations of the team. Mrs. Manley had what proved to be natural business instincts and ownership skills. She did it all: arranged playing schedules, planned team travel, handled payroll, bought equipment, negotiated player contracts, and handled publicity. The team played their home games at Ebbets Field, home of Brooklyn's Major League team, the Dodgers.

After the first season the Manleys realized the team could not survive financially in Brooklyn. They moved across the Hudson River to Newark, New Jersey and bought a black semi-pro team called the Newark Dodgers. They merged it with the team they owned in Brooklyn and began the next season as the Newark Eagles. It proved to be a good move. Newark's black community embraced the team. Former Eagles' pitcher Max Manning said, "The Eagles were to black Newark as the Dodgers were to Brooklyn."

Mrs. Manley did not hesitate to give advice to her managers and players, even though some of it was not well received because it came from a woman. She was very competitive. She hated to lose and frequently addressed the team with outbursts of anger after they lost a game. There are stories of her sitting in the stands, giving the team bunt signals during the game by crossing and uncrossing her legs. There were also rumors of her being romantically involved with some of her players. Supposedly, this is why her husband traded pitcher Terris "Speed" McDuffie to the New York Black Yankees for two old bats and a pair of used sliding pads.

Mrs. Manley strongly believed in improving the conditions for not just her team, but all Negro League players. She spoke out for better scheduling, improved pay, and upgraded facilities. For her team's comfort when travelling on road trips, she purchased a $15,000 air conditioned bus. No other Negro League team travelled in such style. Seen by players as difficult when asked to give salary increases, she still had a generous heart and treated her players like family. She loaned Monte Irvin money to make the down payment on his first home. The Manleys were the godparents of Larry Doby's first child.

Active in the fight against racial discrimination, Mrs. Manley organized in 1934 a boycott of Harlem area stores that refused to hire African American sales clerks. By the next year 300 blacks clerks were working in those stores. An active member of Newark's chapter of the National Association for the Advancement of Colored People (NAACP), she used Eagles' games to bring awareness to civil rights issues, such as having an "Anti-Lynching Day" in 1939.

At league ownership meetings she attended with her husband, Mrs. Manley did not hesitate to go against the other male owners. At first they refused to accept any of her suggestions, but it did not stop her from giving her unsolicited advice and speaking up on important issues. For years the NNL struggled with retaining a strong league commissioner and Mrs. Manley was always in the middle of that on-going fight. She tried to weld her influence against the commissioners she disliked and to support the ones she did. Her husband served as League Treasurer for many years, but the owners all knew who really held the position. Over time the other owners finally stopped seeing her as just a woman and accepted her.

As Mrs. Manley's Eagles were having their Negro League World Series winning season in 1946, former Kansas City Monarchs' shortstop Jackie Robinson was having a great season with the Brooklyn Dodgers' top minor league team in Montreal. Despite Robinson's verbal contract with the Negro League team, Dodgers' General Manager Branch Rickey did not pay one cent for him. Not wanting to be seen as against their players getting a chance to play in the Major Leagues, Negro League club owners were hesitant to criticize Rickey. "We were in no position to protest and Rickey knew it," said Mrs. Manley. But not afraid of being criticized, she eventually spoke out saying black club owners had invested money in the development of their players and should be given compensation if Major League teams wanted them.

In 1947 Mrs. Manley stood behind what she said. The Cleveland Indians purchased Newark Eagles' second baseman Larry Doby for $15,000. Cleveland's transaction with her for Doby also was the first time a Major League team paid a substantial price for a Negro League player. It sent a notice that Negro League players could not be taken without compensating Negro League owners. It set the precedent for future transactions for Negro League players. The money from the Doby transaction allowed Mrs. Manley to keep her team operating that year.

According to Mrs. Manley, "Our troubles started when Jackie Robinson joined the Dodgers." Once Robinson and other African American players went to the Major Leagues, the interest and loyalty of black baseball fans went with them. Attendance at Negro League games declined. Mrs. Manley's Eagles drew 146,000 fans in 1946, but only 35,000 in 1948. When the NNL disbanded after the 1948 season, Mrs. Manley sold her team to a Memphis dentist who moved it to Houston. In the business of professional baseball for 13 years, she knew the time had come to get out of the game.

But shortly after the sale Mrs. Manley angrily protested when Eagles' shortstop Monte Irvin signed with the Brooklyn Dodgers, setting up a battle with Branch Rickey. Due compensation for the signing of any Eagles' player by a Major League team based on a stipulation in selling the team, she threatened to sue the Dodgers. Believing Rickey had stolen Eagles' pitcher Don Newcombe from her years earlier, she determined it would not happen again. Rickey backed away, released Irvin, and Mrs. Manley sold him to the New York Giants for $5,000.

Effa Manley believed the growing economics of baseball drove black owners out of the game and killed the Negro Leagues. After selling her team she said, "Baseball has become a rich man's hobby and we are not rich." She died on April 16, 1981.

When Monte Irvin saw her a few years before her death, he could tell she still had the outgoing style and grand appearance that always made her stand out. He saw her wearing the same mink coat she bought with the money she received for selling him to the Giants 30 years earlier. Irvin told her she made a good buy. She said, "So did the Giants".

In her later years Mrs. Manley continued to be an advocate for the institution of Negro League baseball in which she had spent over 10 years of her life. She co-authored a book, "Negro League Baseball Before Integration." It was about notable Negro League players, many of which played on her team. Mrs. Manley also sent letters to the Hall of Fame suggesting various Negro League players she felt deserved induction, many of which also played on her Newark Eagles. The Hall of Fame did more than accept her suggestions by honoring her with induction in 2006 for all her accomplishments in the game she loved.

CHAPTER 18

Alejandro Pompez

During the "whites only" Major League baseball era there were a few light-skinned Cubans such as Adolfo Luque that crossed the "invisible color line". But they faced racial insults and discrimination from white players that saw them no different in terms of race than African Americans. Faced with these same racial barriers, Hispanics turned to the Negro Leagues to play professional baseball in the United States. This created a common thread between African American and Latin American ballplayers despite their cultural differences. It was a binding thread that lasted throughout the lifetime of Negro League baseball. The main architect of that thread was Alejandro "Alex" Pompez. He created the "Latin Connection" in the Negro Leagues that extended to the Major Leagues after the racial barriers were broken down.

Pompez, a black Cuban American, worked in Negro League baseball for more than 30 years. His first team, the Cuban Stars, barnstormed the eastern United States beginning in 1916. In 1923, the Stars were one of the original teams of the Eastern Color League (ECL), the second official Negro League baseball league formed. It remained a fixture in Negro League baseball throughout the 1920s. After a break from baseball following the 1929 season Pompez returned in 1935 with a new team in the newly formed Negro National League (NNL), the New York Cubans. Once again Negro League baseball had a Latin flavor.

Born of Cuban immigrants on May 3, 1890, Alex Pompez spent his first years in Key West and Tampa, Florida where his father owned cigar manufacturing plants. Being able to speak both English and fluent Spanish allowed Pompez to easily fit in both American and Latin American cultures. After his father's death in 1896 Pompez's mother moved the family to Cuba. Fourteen years later Alex returned to Tampa and worked in the cigar industry. After a short stay, he moved to New York City and opened a cigar store in Harlem.

Pompez acquired his passion for baseball while living in Cuba, where the popularity of the game spiraled as the 20th Century began. The country had gained its independence from Spain in 1902 following the Spanish-American War (1898 – 1902), but struggled under the military control of the United States Army. The close geographical and political ties to the United States were reflected in Cuba's tourism, economy, and its baseball. But unlike in the US, players of all colors were welcome in Cuban winter league baseball. African Americans not only played against Hispanic players, but also against white Major Leaguers. Cuban baseball fans in the early 1900s got to see great African American ballplayers such as Oscar Charleston, John Henry "Pop" Lloyd, Pete Hill, and Louis Santop.

Pompez brought this connection between African American and Hispanic players to American soil beginning in 1916 by organizing a Cuban team that barnstormed through the Northeast. The team, the Cuban Stars, contained mostly dark skinned Cubans that he gave the opportunity to play US baseball rather than work in Cuba's sugar mills. Since most white professional teams refused to play them, the Cuban Stars went up against the best African American teams in the east.

In 1923 Pompez began his over two decade participation in Negro League baseball when his Cuban Stars were one of the original teams in the Eastern Colored League (ECL), the second official Negro baseball league. The Negro National League (NNL) had been formed in 1920. His team finished in second place that first ECL season and he became one of the most influential owners in the league. As the main ECL negotiator, Pompez worked with NNL founder Andrew "Rube" Foster to layout the framework for the first Negro League Baseball World Series in 1924. His high status in Negro League baseball is indicated by the official Negro League World Series photo that year showing him in the middle of the picture between the two teams, the Kansas City Monarchs and Hilldale of Darby, Pennsylvania, along with Rube Foster. It is one of the most famous photos of Negro League baseball that still exists.

That same year the Cuban Stars had a fifteen year old second baseman, Martin Dihigo. The black Cuban played 22 years in the Negro Leagues, mostly with Pompez's teams. Many considered him if not the best all-around player in Negro League baseball, certainly the most versatile. In his career Dihigo played every position on the field, including pitcher. Called "El Immortal" in Cuba meaning "The Immortal One", Dihigo is viewed as Pompez's greatest player contribution to Negro League baseball.

The Cuban Stars remained in the ECL until the league stopped operating before the 1928 season. There were too many teams in the league that could no longer financially stay alive. With the worst economic depression in history beginning in 1929 the NNL disappeared after the 1931 season as Negro League baseball overall faced a financial crisis. Instead of determining how his team would survive, Pompez left baseball to get involved in what would be a more lucrative profession.

Pompez ran a numbers operation in Harlem and was seen as a successful businessman who was good for the community. By 1931 his operation is said to have made $7,000 a day. Some believed him to be the richest man in Harlem. He wore fancy expensive clothes and lived flamboyantly.

But his success came at a price as he associated with people that would cause him future legal problems and threaten his life. To keep his operation protected from law enforcement he associated with corrupt New York City political boss James Hines. His business became so lucrative it got the attention of New York mobster Dutch Schultz who forcibly took it over. Pompez became a part of "the Dutchman's" organized crime organization.

In 1935 he returned to Negro League baseball with a new team. His New York Cubans were a part of the newly formed Negro National League. To survive the economic struggles of the early 1930s, many Negro League teams were funded by numbers operators. Pompez's New York Cubans, the Homestead Grays, Pittsburg Crawfords, New York Black Yankees, and Brooklyn Eagles were all teams in the new NNL whose owners partnered with numbers operators. Even though these partnerships may have appeared inappropriate to some, there is no evidence to show the results of any games were purposely fixed and the fans never lost trust in Negro League baseball due to the number operators' involvement.

Pompez composed his team with a mix of players. There were African Americans and players he recruited from Cuba, Panama, Puerto Rico, and other Latin American countries. Very few Negro League teams owned the stadium where they played. They had to pay fees to use the stadiums of Major League teams. But Pompez had his own field, Dyckman Oval Park. He spent thousands of dollars revitalizing and adding a lighting system to the stadium for night games and also persuaded former Cuban Star Martin Dihigo to manage the team. In the Cubans' first year they finished tied for first with the Pittsburgh Crawfords, a team that had four Hall of Famers: Oscar Charleston, Judy Johnson, Josh Gibson, and "Cool Papa" Bell. The Crawfords beat Pompez's team in a playoff for the NNL championship four games to three.

The other owners gladly welcomed Pompez back to Negro League baseball. He brought a calm statesman like professional approach to addressing many problems. His style worked to counterbalance the outspoken approaches of other owners like the Homestead Grays' Cum Posey and the Newark Eagles' Effa Manley. The other owners respected his knowledge of the games' business side.

However, his past involvement in the numbers operation brought him trouble after the Cubans first year in the NNL. In the spring of 1936 New York City prosecuting attorneys decided to go after James Hines, the political boss who had helped keep numbers operators like Pompez in business. The prosecutors wanted Pompez to testify about Hines and organized crime. They charged him with illegal gambling activities and ordered him before the Grand Jury. Although "Dutch" Schultz had been dead since 1935, Pompez feared for his life and fled the country, first to France and then Mexico. After given a promise of police protection and leniency, he returned to New York in August of 1937. His testimony helped to convict Hines in 1939. Coming out of the entire ordeal with just a suspended sentence and probation, Pompez exclaimed to reporters his dedication to baseball. He said of the nation's pastime, "There may not be much money in it, but it is safer".

The New York Cubans missed the entire 1937 and 1938 seasons due to Pompez's legal problems. However, he had it operating again in 1939. Although Dyckman Oval Park had been demolished, they played games at the New York Giants' Polo Grounds. After finishing below .500 the first two seasons upon returning to the league, the Cubans finished first the second half of the 1941 season but lost in the playoffs to the Homestead Grays. Except for one bad year, 1945, the team remained competitive throughout the war years. Pompez's team had its best year in 1947, winning the NNL pennant and then beating the Cleveland Buckeyes to win the Negro League World Series Championship.

The news of Jackie Robinson breaking through Major League baseball's "invisible color line" overshadowed the Cubans winning their championship in 1947. Like the other Negro League team owners, Pompez had mixed emotions about the line being broken. While glad to see the door allowing African Americans to play baseball in the Major Leagues had finally opened, he also felt apprehensive about the effect it would have on the Negro Leagues. Black baseball fans began to turn their attention to the Major Leagues because of Robinson. Although his team won the championship that year, Pompez lost $20,000 due to a drop in attendance. More African Americans placed more attention on Robinson and the Brooklyn Dodgers playing the New York Yankees in the 1947 Major League World Series than on the Cubans victorious Negro League World Series victory.

Instead of remaining apprehensive about African Americans beginning to play in the Major Leagues, Pompez decided to take action. He had sold two white Cuban players to Major League teams in the 1920s and believed that with the color line being broken, Negro League teams could profit monetarily from being a resource for supplying players. In 1948 he made written overtures to the New York Giants and other Major League teams offering first option on buying any of his players on the New York Cubans. No other Negro League team made such an effort towards Major League clubs. As a result, four of the first five Hispanic players in the Major Leagues were former Pompez players: Orestes "Minnie" Minoso, Rafael "Ray" Noble, Edmunds "Sandy" Amoros, and Hector Rodriguez. In total, Pompez sent seven of his players to the Major Leagues.

The New York Cubans took the field for the last time in 1950. The previous two years had been unprofitable. The NNL had gone out of business and all the team owners Pompez had successfully worked with since the 1930s were all gone. He faced intense competition for attracting black baseball fans because six of the nine black players in the Major Leagues were on New York teams, the Brooklyn Dodgers and New York Giants. After 14 years, Pompez believed it was time to get out and the New York Cubans were no more.

But Alejandro Pompez and his "Latin Connection" continued to operate. After integration Pompez played a key role in getting many Hispanic players into the Major Leagues. He became a long time scout for the New York Giants covering the Caribbean countries searching for talented young players. One of his most prized signings, Orlando Cepeda, became the National League 1958 Rookie of the Year and a Hall of Fame inductee in 1999. Another was Hall of Fame pitcher Juan Marichal.

Alex Pompez's career in Negro League baseball spanned over 34 years (1916 – 1950). He saw most of the great black players and his team played against many of the great black teams in Negro League history. When the National Baseball Hall of Fame decided to give recognition to Negro League baseball, it turned to Pompez for help; appointing him on the first special committee that created the process of selecting Negro League players for Hall of Fame induction. Due to the committee's work, many deserving Negro League players began receiving Hall of Fame honors. But Pompez died on March 15, 1974 and did not see his best player, Martin Dihigo, inducted in 1977.

There were some who questioned Alex Pompez's 2006 induction into Baseball's Hall of Fame because of his ties to organized crime in the 1930s. But his positive impact on the national pastime is undeniable and still visible. Pompez's "Latin Connection" which began in the early years of Negro League baseball paved the way for Hispanic players in American professional baseball. Miquel Cabrera and other Hispanic players of today are products of Alex Pompez's efforts.

CONCLUSION

It is uncertain as to whether any of the other former Negro League players and executives/managers not chosen during the 2006 selection process will be someday elected into the Hall of Fame. Although one, John "Buck" O'Neil, has a statue now at Cooperstown recognizing him as Negro League baseball's greatest ambassador, he did not get selected for induction in 2006 as a player. Also not selected were: "Cannonball" Dick Redding, who some say threw the ball as hard as Hall of Famer "Smokey" Joe Williams; Grant "Home Run" Johnson; Dick Lundy; Newt Allen; C. I. Taylor; or Minnie Minoso who also had an All-Star Major League career. They will be included in the on-going debate along with former Major League players such as Gil Hodges, Roger Maris, and others about who deserves a plaque in Cooperstown

But being a part of the black baseball era should not negatively affect the Negro Leaguers in this debate. Negro League baseball has come from behind the "invisible color line" and is now clearly identified as an everlasting fixture of baseball history. The 17 Hall of Fame inductees from the Negro Leagues that arrived on the train to Cooperstown in 2006 cemented that fact.

Purchase other Black Rose Writing titles at www.blackrosewriting.com/books
and use promo code PRINT to receive a 20% discount.

CPSIA information can be obtained
at www.ICGtesting.com
Printed in the USA
LVOW13s1435030117
519574LV00008B/605/P